Marketing Strategies for Every MBTI Type
A Comprehensive Guide for Authors.

By

Donovan M. Neal

TornVeil

Contents

Chapter One

Understanding the importance of your MBTI temperament type in book marketing

This book is the culmination of a transformative epiphany I experienced while attending a writer's group in May of 2023. In that gathering, I noticed a common plea among the authors: "HELP! How can I effectively promote my book?" The room was filled with suggestions from various authors, including myself, each offering different tactics like building a mailing list or watching a particular video series. It was a cacophony of voices. However, amidst the chaos, I had a realization—I recognized that each person was speaking from their own temperament, and of course from their own experience. This realization became the foundation for the comprehensive list of promotional options based on individual temperament types, which forms the cornerstone of this book.

While conducting extensive research to gauge the broader demand for this information, I realized that I had not come across any book that integrated the premise of how one's temperament can influence authorprenuerial promotional strategies. My decision was to fill this void in the market.

Drawing upon my seven years of teaching experience on temperament, and by exploring the MBTI (Myers-Briggs Type Indicator), and by using the latest AI tool Chat-GPT. I've asked the tool to overlap MBTI profile predilections with ninety-four current promotional tactics available to authors as of this writing, in doing so I was able to compile unique promotional results specific for each MBTI temperament. I present to you now the summation of these results.

The result is a practical book that serves as a launching pad or primer for authors, that enables them to embark on tangible promotional actions aligned with their temperament style. This is crucial because some promotional activities simply clash with your inherent wiring. By understanding why certain marketing efforts feel challenging while others don't, authors can maximize what works best for them, extend their reach, and connect with as many readers as possible; allowing authors to use those tactics that best align with their natural tendencies. Where those promotional options don't align, the information provided within these pages gives authors insight as to what promotional tactics might require outside help or simply provide a different approach to better conform with their style of doing things.

I love the MBTI and I firmly believe it allows a person to obtain valuable insights about oneself and others, fosters personal growth, improves relationships, and enhances decision-making in both personal and professional contexts. My goal is to harness this power and direct it towards your authorprenuerial promotional aspirations.

My hypothesis is that many authors who struggle with the authorpreneurship process, particularly book promotion, do so because they may unknowingly be fighting against their own temperament. You are essentially warring against yourself and thus swimming upstream. I conjecture that many of us simply have not discovered how to align our authorpreneurship marketing actions with our temperament. This resistance or "brain fog," can create overwhelming confusion regarding which promotional tactics to pursue. Again, your actions (or those that are recommended by the experts in authorpreneurship) are simply going against the grain of who you are.

If any of this remotely resonates with you, then this book is tailor-made for your needs. I hope to demystify the process of starting the promotion journey and provide initial prompts that direct you towards actions that align best with your unique style. Armed with this knowledge, I trust that you can embark on a successful marketing strategy for your book, empowering you to achieve your book's goals.

My goal with this book is to equip you with the tools you need to navigate the promotional landscape with confidence. Whether you're a seasoned writer or just starting out, this book will be your trusted companion on the path to success, provide practical guidance and personalized insights

The multiple benefits to understanding one's MBTI type.

Knowing one's MBTI (Myers-Briggs Type Indicator) type can be a useful tool for authors looking for efficient marketing techniques because it provides numerous advantages for developing oneself, can assist with creating stronger relationships, and improve decision-making. By delving into the many parts of your personality, we can find insights that point us in the direction of promotional strategies that complement your temperament style the best, maximize your marketing efforts, and more effectively influence your target audience.

Knowing your MBTI type can give you a deep understanding of your inherent promotional style. It can reveal your innate propensities for expression, communication, and innovation. For instance, introverted writers may prefer marketing methods that focus on written content generation, whereas extroverted writers might prefer networking and public speaking. As an author, you should always adjust your promotional efforts to leverage your strengths and magnify your message in a way that connects with your audience in an authentic way by being aware of your innate tendencies.

Additionally, knowing your MBTI type can improve your ability to engage readers more deeply. You can modify your promotional techniques to successfully engage and interact with various segments by knowing the various personality types within your target audience. Authors who are more methodical and analytical might, for instance, create educational blog articles or offer in-depth evaluations of their work, appealing to readers who value intellectual stimulation. Authors who are more intuitive and creative, on the other hand, might concentrate on developing aesthetically appealing content or employing storytelling strategies to arouse their audience's emotions. It's totally possible to build better reader relationships, encourage loyalty, and draw in a more devoted following by matching your promotional strategies with the tastes and inclinations of your readers.

However, there's more! Knowing your MBTI type helps us choose promotional strategies that complement your disposition. For instance, authors who value structure and organization may succeed by creating thorough marketing strategies, meticulously preparing social media postings, and setting up book launch parties. Authors who value spontaneity and adaptability, on the other hand, might favor innovative tactics like viral marketing campaigns or interactive internet events. Understanding your temperament and preferences allows us to identify the promotional methods that feel most authentic and energizing to us, enabling us to approach marketing tasks with enthusiasm and confidence. All of these things can reduce burnout and make marketing less of a chore that we avoid and more of a motivator as we journey on our author careers.

Furthermore, knowing your MBTI type can help you to use your distinctive advantages in your promotion endeavors. For instance, authors who value intuition and foresight may be particularly good at seeing developing trends and capitalizing on them. They could be skilled at spotting industry trends or leveraging social media channels to interact creatively with their audience. Analytically inclined authors may thrive at market research, and data analysis to determine the most efficient promotional channels, or compare the ROI of various strategies. I'm going to emphasize the next point so that it becomes ingrained. You can enhance your effect and the success of your marketing initiatives by coordinating your promotional activities with your inherent strengths.

Remember that knowing your MBTI type not only has many advantages for your personal development, relationships, and decision-making, but it also offers you helpful insights into your promotional activities. You can strengthen your promotional efforts, build deeper relationships with readers, and ultimately boost the effectiveness of your book promotion by matching your marketing techniques with the personalities, strengths, and preferences of your target market. Because of increased self-awareness, it can be easier to negotiate the complicated world of promotion with honesty, excitement, and the knowledge that you are making the right choices for your particular personality and style.

Overview of the Book's Structure and Purpose

This book is a thorough instruction manual made to help you use your MBTI temperament type to improve your book marketing efforts. My opinion is that you may successfully navigate the wide range of promotional strategies and tailor your efforts to better resonate with you and your target audience by understanding the subtleties of your temperament.

The book's framework is set up to enable a step-by-step investigation of each temperament type, enabling you to make wise choices and begin the process of launching successful advertising campaigns suited to your particular tastes and styles.

In the book's introduction, the significance of comprehending one's MBTI temperament type in the context of book marketing is emphasized. It highlights how matching promotional tactics with your temperament can result in more impact, deeper reader connections, and improved success in achieving marketing objectives.

The book then goes into great detail about the four components of the MBTI framework—extraversion/introversion, sensing/intuition, thinking/feeling, and judging/perceiving. The goal here is that by having this fundamental understanding, you can effectively examine and determine your own temperament type.

We'll then take the time to thoroughly examine each temperament type. If you are an Extroverted (E) author you will learn unique book marketing strategies that play to your strengths because you thrive on social contacts and outside stimulation. If you are an author who is introverted (I), who draws their motivation from inside, you will discover techniques that fit with your tastes for more personal and attentive interaction with readers.

The book also discusses book marketing strategies appropriate for authors who prefer to write intuitively or sensibly (S or N). Sensing authors will learn about promotional strategies that place an emphasis on visual appeal, local participation, and concrete information. Sensing authors have a tendency to be careful and practical. Authors with an intuitive writing style are creative and future-focused and as such will find strategies that center on storytelling, specialized marketing, and engaging audiences in more abstract and inventive ways.

The evaluation of thinking (T) and feeling (F) authors is the next step in the investigation of book marketing strategies. Finding advice on emphasizing the logical components of their work, applying data-driven tactics, and outlining clear benefits to possible readers can be helpful for thinking authors who appreciate logic and rationality. On the other side, feeling authors will discover how to highlight emotional journeys, encourage dialogue, and tie their marketing initiatives to human experiences to build genuine connections with their audience.

The book then covers the book marketing tactics suitable for judging (J) and perceiving (P) authors. If you are a Judging author who enjoys structure and order you will learn methods for putting together well-organized marketing strategies, using scheduling software, and looking for endorsements to establish credibility. Perceiving authors will investigate tactics that promote spontaneity, involvement with readers, and staying aware of market trends for timely modifications. They will embrace flexibility and adaptation.

The book explores a variety of temperament-based book marketing strategies and provides a plethora of tools to aid authors in their promotion efforts and offers authors a wide choice of possibilities to pick from based on their preferences and marketing objectives thanks to the extensive list of 94 advertising tactics I have included. Additionally, there is a quick reference to MBTI promotional prompts that you can use to adapt your promotional efforts and generate ideas.

A thorough reflection on the importance of knowing the MBTI temperament of those readers who make up the genre that you write in is also included in the book's conclusion. In this section, I will emphasize not just the need of matching promotional initiatives with one's innate tastes and tendencies so that your efforts feel genuine and in line with their individual style but also show how you can market to the MBTI types of those you might most comprise your genres market. This information will let you see where you are hitting resistance in trying to promote your work.

In conclusion, the goal of this book is to arm you with the information and resources you will need to make the most of your MBTI temperament type in your book marketing campaigns. I hope to increase your chances of success in attracting your preferred readership by creating a tailored and successful marketing approach that fits with how your temperament influences your promotional preferences. Now having said all this, if you do not know your MBTI temperament type; stop reading now and take the test to find out at https://www.16personalities.comOnce you find out and read up and see if the results describe you then come back and finish reading the rest of the book to take advantage of the information within.

What is the MBTI?

The Myers-Briggs Type Indicator® (MBTI) is a widely used personality assessment tool developed by Katherine Cook Briggs and her daughter, Isabel Briggs Myers. It is based on the work of renowned psychologist Carl Jung and his theory of psychological types.

The MBTI framework is composed of four dimensions or dichotomies, each of which represents a core personality trait. These characteristics capture differences in how people perceive the world, gather information, make decisions, and interact with the outside environment, assisting in the classification of people into various types.

Extraversion (E) and introversion (I) make up the first dimension. It describes the sources of people's energy and their interactions with the outside environment. Extraverts like social contacts, get their energy from outside stimuli and frequently speak their thoughts out. They are frequently characterized as extroverted, gregarious, and expressive. Contrarily, introverts draw strength from their inner world and value isolation and reflection. They frequently need alone time to refuel their energies and have a tendency to consider before they speak.

Sensing (S) against Intuition (N) makes up the second dimension. It illustrates how people choose to learn about the world and view it. Sensing personalities concentrate on specific, observable details and rely on their senses to get knowledge. They value knowledge that is grounded on facts and verifiable data, are careful, and are practical. On the other hand, intuitive people tend to think more symbolically and abstractly. They delve deeper, looking for connections, patterns, and opportunities. They are imaginative, focused on the future, and frequently let their instincts help them make decisions.

Thinking (T) against Feeling (F) make up the third dimension. It explains how people analyze information and make judgments. Thinking people place a high value on logic, objectivity, and reason. They aim for justice and uniformity while basing choices on objective standards. The importance of one's own ideals, feelings, and how decisions affect other people are prioritized by feeling kinds, in contrast. They base their decisions on their own sentiments and are sympathetic to the feelings of those involved.

The fourth dimension contrasts perception and judgment (J/P). It speaks to how people prefer to spend their lives and interact with the outside world. Organization, structure, and closure are important to judges. They appreciate making decisions and prefer timetables and plans that are clear. They have a tendency to be quick to make decisions and are typically effective in doing so. On the other hand, perceiving personality types respect adaptability, spontaneity, and openness. They enjoy investigating options, are adaptable to new information, and want to keep their options open. They are frequently characterized as adaptive, flexible, and flow-oriented.

Within the MBTI paradigm, these four dimensions collectively create 16 different personality types. There are two possible preferences for each dimension (E or I, S or N, T or F, J or P), giving rise to a total of 16 possible combinations. These mixtures provide a diverse range of personality types, each with its own advantages, preferences, and traits.

Your ability to understand the variety of personalities and successfully navigate interpersonal dynamics depends on your ability to comprehend these dimensions and the combinations derived from them. Once you know your own temperament type, you recognize your strengths and weaknesses and adjust your book promotion tactics to suit you accordingly.

Chapter Two

Understanding the MBTI Temperament Types

A **brief explanation of the MBTI framework and its four dimensions**
Understanding how your personality affects your book advertising techniques is essential for authors. You can better understand yourself and make wise judgments about your promotional strategy by using the MBTI framework, which offers insightful information about your preferences and tendencies.

Let's revisit the entire framework while keeping authorpreneurship in mind. Extraversion (E) and Introversion (I) make up the first MBTI dimension. Extraverted writers enjoy interacting with readers and other writers, and they do well in social situations. By participating actively on social media platforms, planning book launches, and working with influencers, you may take advantage of your innate desire for external stimuli. Conversely, if you tend to be more introverted, you could like more personal and deliberate exchanges. Effective advertising strategies for you may include creating an online presence through websites and blogs, communicating with others directly through email newsletters, and taking part in online writing communities.

How you gather and analyze information depends on the second dimension, Sensing (S) vs. Intuition (N). If you prefer sensation, you are probably practical and detail-oriented. Concrete information seekers will be attracted by visual marketing that uses eye-catching visuals, interactions with neighborhood bookstores, libraries, and newspapers, and the provision of thorough descriptions and reviews. You're imaginative and for-ward-looking thinking opens up possibilities for innovative promotional techniques for individuals with an intuitive inclination. A compelling tale behind your book, storytelling through blog posts, videos, and podcasts, as well as focusing on niche markets and online communities, can all be effective strategies to engage readers.

The Thinking (T) vs. Feeling (F) dimension comes into play while deciding how to promote your book. Thinking authors emphasize reason and reasoning. Your strategy is in line with emphasizing the logical parts of your work, using data-driven techniques, and providing clear benefits and value propositions to potential readers. On the other hand, feeling authors respect subjective knowledge and sentimental ties. You can connect with your audience by emphasizing emotional journeys in your book promotion, having interactions with readers to create a feeling of community, working with nonprofits, or even just donating revenues.

Lastly, the Judging (J) vs. Perceiving (P) dimension affects how you approach the outside world and structure your promotional efforts. If you lean towards judging, you appreciate structure and organization. Creating a well-organized and structured mar-keting plan, utilizing scheduling and productivity tools, and seeking endorsements and testimonials to establish credibility are effective strategies for you. For authors with a perceiving preference, flexibility and adaptability are key. Embrace spontaneity in your interactions with readers, utilize social listening tools to stay attuned to market trends, and make adjustments accordingly.

Last but not least, the Judging (J) vs. Perceiving (P) dimension has an impact on how you interact with the outside world and organize your marketing initiatives. If you have a tendency to toa judging, you value organization and structure. Your best bets for building credibility are to arrange and structure your marketing plan, using scheduling and pro-ductivity tools, and look for endorsements and testimonials. Writers with a perceptual preference will prefer flexibility and adaptation. Essential elements In your interactions with readers, embrace spontaneity. Use social listening tools to be aware of market trends and make adjustments as necessary.

Extraverted (E) vs. Introverted (I)

Key personality traits that affect how authors engage with the outside world and refuel include extraversion and introversion. For writers who favor extraversion, social situations are ideal, and you get your energy from the environment. This indicates that you take pleasure in conversing with readers, authors, and anybody else who expresses interest in your work. Vibrant talks, networking opportunities, and public appearances give you energy. Knowing your temperament type as an extraverted author might help you make the most of your innate need for social engagement outside of your immediate environment to promote your books.

Consider using social media platforms for active involvement to successfully advertise your book. Utilize social media sites like Twitter, Facebook, Instagram, and LinkedIn to interact with your target audience, provide book updates, and participate in discussions about your specialty. Accept invitations to book signings, workshops, and launch events so you may meet readers in person, respond to their inquiries, and develop a following of devoted fans. Working with writers and influencers in your genre might help you gain more exposure and expand your readership.

On the other hand, if you tend to be an introverted writer, you draw your energy from within and frequently require some alone time to refuel. This is just a preference for quieter, more private conversations; it doesn't mean you lack social skills or do not like people. Understanding your temperament type is essential for creating promotional techniques that complement your introverted writing style.

For introverted authors, creating an online presence through websites and blogs can be a useful tool. Establish a personal website so that viewers may find out more about you and your work. Keep a blog where you may post observations, behind-the-scenes tales, and insightful information about the themes of your book. Through email newsletters and private chat, interact one-on-one with your audience to establish a more personal connection. Join online writing groups and forums where you may share insightful commentary, demonstrate your knowledge, and draw readers who identify with your writing style.

Understanding your temperament type will help you negotiate the world of book promotion with greater self-awareness, whether you tend toward extraversion or introversion. It helps you to customize your campaigns to your particular abilities and preferences, resulting in more genuine and successful marketing initiatives.

The next sentence will be repeated several times because I want to drive home my point. In terms of book promotion, keep in mind that there is no correct or wrong temperament type. Each type has a unique set of advantages and strengths. Find marketing strategies that speak to you personally, play to your strengths, and embrace your unique personality. In addition to enjoying the process more, you'll connect with your target audience in a more impactful and real way, improving your chances of success in book promotion and aligning your promotional activities with your temperament.

Sensing (S) vs. Intuitive (N)

Different ways of detecting and obtaining information from the environment are represented by sensing and intuition. Authors who identify with the Sensing preference have a grounded and practical approach. They frequently concentrate on specifics, facts, and experiences from the actual world. Sensing authors have a high sense of detail and thrive in the here and now. They thrive at creating realistic environments, capturing rich sensory details, and giving readers relatable situations.

Consider including eye-catching graphics and images in your book promotion if you have a Sensing preference. Utilize visual networks like Pinterest and Instagram where you may display eye-catching images that perfectly represent the spirit of your book. Work with your local bookstores, libraries, and newspapers to plan live events or book signings so that readers can see and touch your work. People that value specific information and useful benefits will be drawn to your extensive descriptions and reviews. You may effectively express the worth of your book and build a close relationship with your target market by catering to the demands of Sensing readers.

The abstract, symbolic, and imaginative are preferred literary devices among authors that incline toward intuition. They are happiest when pondering about possibilities, patterns, and the future. The ability to integrate different ideas perceive the larger picture, and venture into unexplored territory is a special talent of intuitive authors. They are experts at crafting storylines that make readers think, reveal hidden meanings, and spark their imaginations.

As an intuitive writer, think about applying your storytelling abilities to a variety of platforms. To engage your audience and spark interest in your books, create captivating storylines for your blog posts, videos, and podcasts. Target online communities and niche audiences who identify with the subjects and concepts you investigate. Discuss abstract ideas in your writing to get readers to think critically and connect with your work on a deeper level. Your audience's intuitive inclinations can help you build a devoted following, foster a sense of connection, and inspire people.

Knowing whether you are more Sensing or Intuitive can assist you as a writer to better target your marketing efforts to connect with your target audience. You can modify your communication style, visuals, and content to appeal to the sensing or intuitive side of your audience by determining which group they fall into.

When it comes to book advertising, keep in mind that there is no right or wrong selection. For writers, Sensing and Intuition both present special advantages and opportunities. Aim for the Sensing or Intuitive preferences of your target audience while embracing your natural inclination, playing to your skills, and coming up with innovative ways to convey the substance of your book. Your efforts may establish a solid connection, pique readers' interests, and persuade them to read more of your work.

Thinking (T) vs. Feeling (F)

Now let's take a closer look at the Thinking (T) vs. Feeling (F) temperament types inside the MBTI framework, with an emphasis on how authors may better comprehend and make use of this feature to support their book promotion efforts.

Different decision-making processes and information evaluation methods are represented by Thinking and Feeling. The logic, objectivity, and rationality of their approach are frequently prioritized by authors that lean toward the Thinking preference. They are excellent in data analysis, breaking down challenging ideas, and organizing information. Thinking authors are adept at emphasizing the logical components of their work and demonstrating the useful advantages it provides to readers.

Consider highlighting the logical and rational features of your book in your promotion if you consider yourself a Thinking author. Display the research, facts, and logical justifications that back up your claims. Use data-driven tactics to target your marketing initiatives, such as surveying customers or gathering reader reviews to substantiate your promises. Provide prospective readers with specific advantages and value propositions that demonstrate how your book can address issues, offer new perspectives, or enhance their quality of life. You can gain credibility and position yourself as an authority on your subject by appealing to the rational minds of your audience.

On the other hand, writers who favor the Feeling preference use a more subjective and sympathetic approach to making decisions. Personal ideals, feelings, and the effect their work has on others are given priority. Feeling writers are masters at establishing emotional bonds with their audience, arousing empathy, and offering relevant experiences.

Consider stressing the emotional journey and personal experiences connected to your book in your promotion if you have a Feeling preference. Write realistic, sincere stories that touch your readers' innermost feelings. Create a sense of community and connection by conversing with your audience. Join forces with nonprofits or give a portion of the book's sales to causes that share your values. You can develop a devoted and devoted following by emphasizing the emotional impact of your work and encouraging empathy.

Understanding your individual preference for Thinking or Feeling can be really helpful in determining your promotion techniques as an author. You may adjust your messaging, tone, and content to appeal to your target audience's preferences by being aware of their preferences. Understanding the Thinking and Feeling preferences enables you to engage with your readers on a deeper level, whether you are appealing to their rational minds or their heartstrings.

Thinking and Feeling both have distinctive advantages and possibilities. Find genuine methods to connect with your readers by embracing your natural inclinations, playing to your strengths, and using your voice. You may evoke strong emotional connections and motivate your target audience to interact with your work on a meaningful level by recognizing and aligning with their preferences for Thinking or Feeling.

Judging (J) vs. Perceiving (P)

Let's begin a thorough investigation of the MBTI framework's Judging (J) versus Perceiving (P) temperament types, with a focus on how authors may comprehend and make use of this feature to improve their book promotion efforts.

Judging and Perceiving indicate various approaches to the outside world and methods of structuring one's life, similar to the aforementioned temperaments. Judging-preference writers frequently place a high emphasis on preparation, structure, and order. Schedules, deadlines, and a clear sense of direction are essential to their success. Judging authors are excellent at organizing and structuring their marketing strategies in order to make sure that their book promotion is successful. Consider using your preference for structure and organization in your promotional methods if you consider yourself a Judging author. Make a marketing strategy with well-defined goals, deadlines, and doable activities. To keep on track and accomplish your goals, use scheduling and productivity tools. To create credibility and win the audience's trust, ask significant people in your sector for recommendations and testimonials. You may inspire confidence in potential readers and pique their interest in your book by showcasing your dedication to a well-thought-out concept.

Authors who favor Perceiving, on the other hand, frequently value spontaneity, flexibility, and adaptability. Exploration, improvisation, and seizing possibilities as they present themselves are what they thrive on. Perceiving authors excel at making quick decisions, being adaptable, and having impromptu conversations with their readers.

Consider embracing the fluidity of your creative process in your book promotion if you have a Perceiving inclination. Accept the freedom to modify your marketing strategy in response to changing consumer and market demands. Use social media to engage in spontaneous encounters with your readers by answering questions and starting discussions. Utilize social listening techniques to stay abreast of industry trends and modify your promotion methods as necessary. You may develop a dynamic and interesting promotional strategy that piques the interest of your target audience by utilizing your adaptability and grasping opportunities as they present themselves.

Knowing whether you judge or see things differently can help you as an author to better target your marketing efforts and connect with readers. Always tailor your marketing strategy to meet the demands and preferences of your target audience by being aware of their preferences.

I know I've said it before but it bears continuously repeating that when it comes to book advertising, there is no right or wrong approach; each temperament presents particular advantages and opportunities for authors. Play to your strengths, embrace your natural inclinations, and come up with original ways to get your audience's attention. You may develop an engaging and effective book promotion that connects with your target audience on a personal level by becoming aware of and connecting with their Judging or Perceiving preferences.

Chapter Three

Extraverted (E) Book Marketing Tactics

Extraverted (E) book marketing tactics are methods for promoting a book that makes use of active participation and outward connections, with an emphasis on outside platforms and communities. These strategies work well for authors who are energized by social connections and excel in the outside world. Here are some extraverted book marketing tactics.

Use Social Media Platforms: To connect with readers, other authors, and influential people in your field, actively take part on social media sites like Facebook, Twitter, Instagram, and LinkedIn. Share novel-related news, behind-the-scenes information, and insights. To establish a strong online presence and establish a connection with your target audience, reply to comments and take part in debates.

Organize Workshops, Book Signings, and Launch Events: Plan and host live events like book launches, signings, and seminars to promote your book. Face-to-face interactions with readers, book signings, and other memorable experiences are all important. Utilize online event platforms, neighborhood bookstores, and community centers to plan events and draw attendees.

Partner with Authors and Influencers: Find authors and influencers who have comparable target markets or shared interests. Join forces through blog pieces, guest interviews, promotional events, or social media takeovers to grow your audience and reach. This partnership may introduce your book to new audiences and increase interest in it.

Attend author panels and give speeches in public: Look for chances to take part in author panels, public appearances, and literary festivals. Discuss the subjects of your book, share your knowledge, and interact with the audience. You can gain exposure to a larger audience at these events and develop your expertise in your field.

Make fascinating Book Trailers and films: Make book trailers and films by utilizing the power of visual storytelling. These can be disseminated through websites, social media platforms, and video-sharing services like YouTube. Entice viewers with visuals, a brief description, and excerpts from reviews..

Establish a mailing list of interested readers and send newsletters periodically. Share privileged information, updates, and limited-time deals concerning your book. In order to manage your subscriber list and gauge engagement, use email marketing services.

Take part in Guest Blogging and Article Writing: Write articles for industry journals or relevant websites as a guest blogger. By doing so, you can connect with a larger audience and establish your expertise. To increase traffic and spark curiosity, include a biography and a link to your book in your author byline.

These are only a few illustrations of extraverted book marketing strategies. The secret is to actively interact with readers, influential people in the business, and different venues to promote your book and build buzz about it. You can reach a wider audience, make relationships, and establish a firm presence in the literary world by adopting these tactics.

Chapter Four

Introverted (I) Book Marketing Tactics

A uthors that prefer a more introspective, individualized approach to book promotion may benefit from using introverted (I) book marketing tactics. The following strategies emphasize developing an online presence, human interactions, and participation in more quiet settings. The following are some illustrations of introverted book marketing strategies:

Create a professional author website or blog where you can promote your book, post updates, and offer insights into your writing process to establish an online presence. This enables introverted authors to communicate with a worldwide audience in a more regulated and comfortable setting.

Use private messaging and email newsletters to interact with people one-on-one: Create a mailing list, and then send your readers individualized email newsletters. This enables you to have a close relationship with your audience and share exclusive content, insider information, and promotional offers. React to individual emails and private communications to promote a feeling of intimacy and devotion.

Join online writing communities, forums, and social media groups created especially for authors and readers to participate in online writing communities and forums. Participate in debates, impart advice, and assist other authors. This gives you the chance to interact with people who have similar interests to yours and potential readers.

Create online workshops, Q&A sessions, or book clubs where you may communicate with readers in a more relaxed, introvert-friendly environment. These gatherings give you a stage for more in-depth conversations where you can discuss the topics, observations, and personal experiences of your book.

Focus on Book Reviews and suggestions: Ask people to give your book reviews and suggestions on websites like Goodreads, Amazon, or book blogs. To develop attention and credibility, introverted authors can take advantage of social proof and word-of-mouth marketing strategies. Engage with readers who post reviews, expressing appreciation and offering extra details.

Write Meaningful Content: Introverted authors frequently excel at writing thoughtful, meaningful content. Write in-depth blog posts, essays, or articles about the subjects of your book or the writing process. Share with your target audience relevant personal experiences, reflections, or professional viewpoints. You can demonstrate your knowledge and establish a stronger connection with readers with this kind of content.

Create Connections with Bloggers and Book Reviewers: Speak with bloggers, influencers, and book reviewers who are interested in your genre or intended audience. In exchange for a frank review or feature, offer them a free copy of your book. Through these connections, you can reach a larger audience and gain access to reputable reviews while promoting your book.

Introverted book marketing techniques emphasize establishing trusting relationships, cultivating a feeling of community, and using more reflective promotional techniques. Introverted authors can develop a devoted and devoted fan base by utilizing these techniques while still striking a comfortable balance between offline encounters and online presence.

Chapter Five

Sensing (S) Book Marketing Tactics

The marketing tactics and techniques employed for Sensing (S) are centered on interacting with readers through real-world situations. They place a strong emphasis on using traditional marketing channels, giving precise information, and drawing attention through visual appeal. The following are some examples of such book marketing strategies:

Sensing-focused marketing strategies frequently make use of visually arresting graphics and imagery to draw the reader's attention. This can involve developing captivating book covers, eye-catching social media posts, and employing top-notch imagery in advertising materials. The objective is to grab the reader's interest and deliver a crystal-clear message on the book's substance.

Participate in Local Newspapers, Libraries, and Bookstores: Sensing-oriented marketing techniques involve actively interacting with nearby bookshops, libraries, and publications to advertise the book. This can entail planning book signings, taking part in author events, obtaining local media coverage, and conspicuously displaying the book in public spaces where readers can find it.

Give Detailed Reviews and Descriptions: Sensing-oriented authors are aware that some readers value specific details and in-depth descriptions of the book's substance. Readers that seek a more factual and concrete grasp of what they can expect from the book will find that they focus on offering full book summaries, detailed chapter breakdowns, and exhaustive evaluations that highlight particular features of the book.

Use Conventional Marketing Channels: Sensing-focused authors can make use of conventional marketing channels like print publications, radio interviews, and direct mail campaigns. They are aware that some readers still interact with these conventional media and respect printed information. This may entail publishing advertisements in pertinent periodicals or newspapers, arranging radio discussions of the book, or distributing direct mail advertisements to certain groups of people.

Sensible book marketing strategies generally involve participating in regional gatherings and book fairs where writers can interact with readers face-to-face. Authors can do this to promote their works, engage potential readers in demonstrations or interactive experiences, and personally engage with them. These in-person contacts establish a real bond between the writer and the readers.

In order to pique the interest of consumers who prefer a more concrete and factual approach to discovering books, Sensing Book Marketing Tactics emphasize presenting solid facts, engaging with readers through visual appeal and traditional methods, and offering thorough descriptions.

Chapter Six

Intuitive (N) Book Marketing Tactics

T he goal of intuitive (N) book marketing tactics and methods is to pique readers' interest and attention through originality, compelling storytelling, and the targeting of certain niches. They place a strong emphasis on building suspense, appealing to emotions, and using creative promotional methods. The following are some illustrations of intuitive book marketing strategies:

Create a Compelling Story: Intuitive writers are aware of the ability of storytelling to capture readers' attention. They create an engaging story about their book, stressing its original idea, surprising twists, or underlying themes. This can be accomplished by enticing readers with intriguing book summaries, interesting author interviews, or intriguing video trailers.

Participate in Storytelling in a Variety of Media: Utilizing a variety of media to engage readers through narrative is a component of intuitively oriented marketing techniques. This can involve working with authors to develop aesthetically appealing visuals or animations that bring the book to life, producing engrossing films or podcasts that explore the book's themes, or writing blog articles that give personal tales or insights relating to it.

Target niche demographics and online communities: Target marketing is important for intuitive authors who want to reach readers who will connect with their book. They participate actively in online forums, social media organizations, and communities that cater to their particular interests. Authors can position themselves as authorities in their field, draw readers who are truly interested in their book, and establish themselves as experts by taking part in pertinent discussions, offering insights, and producing important content.

Leverage Viral Marketing and Memes: Using viral trends and memes to create buzz and draw in a larger audience are possible intuitive book marketing strategies. Authors can capitalize on the collective curiosity and interest of online communities by developing memorable slogans, taking part in well-liked social media challenges, or using trending themes.

Work together with bloggers and influencers: Astute authors are aware of the effectiveness of influential voices in reaching their target audience. They aggressively work with online influencers in their particular area or genre, such as book bloggers, bookstagrammers, or social media personalities. Authors can take advantage of these influencers' audience and reputation by providing advanced copies of the book for reviews, presenting guest blog posts, or engaging in collaborative marketing initiatives.

Use technology to engage with readers through the hosting of virtual events and webinars. They arrange online book premieres, author Q&A sessions, or interactive seminars that let readers connect with the author directly and delve further into the topics and concepts of the book. These online gatherings offer a chance to develop a readership that is active and to generate excitement for the book.

In general, intuitive book marketing strategies place a higher priority on creativity, storytelling, and the identification of niche audiences through a variety of media and cutting-edge advertising platforms. They want to arouse interest, engage readers' emotions, and produce an immersive experience that appeals to their craving for something distinctive and engrossing.

Chapter Seven

Thinking (T) Book Marketing Tactics

T hinking (T) Book Marketing Tactics and Strategies emphasize the use of data-driven tactics, logical arguments, and displaying the worth of the book to draw readers. They place a high priority on communicating the book's advantages, offering insightful analysis, and making use of techniques that appeal to a logical and impartial perspective. Following are some illustrations of Thinking Book marketing strategies:

Thinking-oriented authors place special emphasis on the logical and reasonable components of their books in their marketing campaigns. They **concentrate on making succinct and understandable arguments that highlight the intellectual value of the book and captivate readers who seek factual information.** This can be accomplished by writing well-organized book descriptions, emphasizing essential ideas or arguments, and showcasing the book's original insights or research-based methodology.

Employ data-driven strategies: Astute authors may use data-driven approaches to advertise their books. They use market analysis, analytics software, and reader feedback to influence their judgments about focusing on a particular demographic or customizing their promotional strategies. This may entail gathering information through surveys or polls, examining sales data to spot patterns, or doing keyword research to increase internet presence.

Offer Clearly Stated Benefits and Value Propositions: Thinking-oriented marketing strategies call for stating the book's benefits and value propositions in a distinctly articulate manner. Authors emphasize how their book helps readers by addressing an issue, offering helpful advice, or educating them. This might be accomplished by employing catchy taglines, succinct explanations of the main points, or endorsements that highlight the significance of the work.

Leverage Credible Endorsements: Smart authors understand the value of establishing their expertise and reputation in their marketing. They look for recommendations from authorities, professionals, or well-known personalities in the subject area of their book. Endorsements aid in establishing confidence and reassure readers that the book offers trustworthy and worthwhile information.

Use Analytical Platforms and Tools: Authors who value analysis can use analytical platforms and tools to monitor and evaluate the results of their marketing initiatives. To gauge the success of their marketing initiatives, they track indicators, including website traffic, click-through rates, conversion rates, and social media engagement. Authors may make well-informed judgments and improve their marketing strategy with this data-driven method for improved outcomes.

Actively participate in industry gatherings and conferences that touch on the subject of their books. Thinking authors present research findings, take part in roundtable discussions, or make instructive presentations that highlight their subject-matter knowledge. Authors can become thought leaders and entice readers who appreciate intellectual conversation by exhibiting their expertise and networking with experts in their subject.

In order to draw readers, Thinking Book Marketing Tactics places a strong emphasis on logical thinking, data-driven decision-making, and offering distinct value propositions. Authors can entice readers who are looking for well-reasoned and useful content by highlighting the book's intellectual merit, using statistics and analytics, and leveraging authoritative endorsements.

Chapter Eight

Feeling (F) Book Marketing Tactics

Making emotional connections, highlighting personal experiences, and developing a feeling of community among readers are the main goals of Feeling (F) book marketing tactics and methods. They place a high value on engaging readers' emotions, emphasizing the book's influence on readers' relationships and personal growth, and implementing techniques that connect with readers on a more profound, sincere level. Examples of marketing strategies for the book "Feeling" are as follows:

Emphasize Emotional Journeys: Authors that are emotionally intelligent are aware of the need of evoking strong feelings in their readers. They emphasize the emotional journeys that are portrayed in their book, whether it is a story that is heartwarming, an account of overcoming adversity, or one that inspires empathy. They place special emphasis on the characters' challenges, emotions, and the potential for readers to undergo transformation. This can be accomplished by using moving book summaries, moving quotes, or testimonies that highlight the book's emotional impact.

Talk to Readers and Create Communities: Feeling authors place a high priority on talking to readers and creating communities around their books. They take part in online debates on social media, reply to reader comments, and conduct live chats or online book clubs. Authors strengthen the emotional connection between readers and their books by developing a sense of community and providing a secure environment for readers to express their ideas and experiences.

Partner with Charitable Organizations: Feeling marketing strategies may include working with nonprofits or donating a portion of book sales to deserving causes. Readers that appreciate having a positive impact on the world can relate to this. Authors can advertise their books as ways to help a greater good by connecting the themes or messages in them with pertinent topics.

Use compelling imagery and symbolism in their book marketing materials. Authors that write with a strong emotional connection often design visually appealing book covers, employ metaphorical language, or include significant symbols that convey the depth of emotion in their writing. Authors can captivate readers' interest and pique their curiosity by appealing to their imagination and evoking emotional associations.

Share Personal Experiences and Vulnerability: Authors that use feeling-oriented marketing strategies share personal experiences and stories that touch readers emotionally. They might create blog posts or social media content that discusses their own writing experience, the sources of inspiration for the book, or unique anecdotes connected to the subjects of the book. Authors establish confidence and establish a sincere relationship with readers by being vulnerable.

Encourage Reader Testimonials and Reviews: Feeling authors actively look for reader reviews and testimonials that capture the impact of their book on the reader's emotions. They invite readers to express their opinions, sentiments, and unique connections to the narrative. These endorsements act as significant social proof and can connect with potential readers who respect other people's real-world experiences.

The overall goals of Feeling Book Marketing Tactics are to evoke strong emotions, build a feeling of community, and place an emphasis on close relationships with readers. Authors can draw readers who are looking for works that touch their emotions and provide a deeper, more meaningful reading experience by focusing on emotional journeys, participating in conversations, and using important symbolism.

Chapter Nine

Judging (J) Book Marketing Tactics

In order to effectively promote and position the book in the market, judging (J) book marketing tactics and methods place a strong emphasis on planning, organization, and structure. In order to make sure that the book reaches its intended readership and is successful, they place a high priority on meticulous planning, clearly defined objectives, and methodical procedures. Here are a few illustrations of marketing strategies for judging books:

Make a Strategic Marketing Plan: Judging-oriented authors create a thorough marketing strategy that details particular tactics, deadlines, and objectives. They establish specific objectives, pinpoint target populations, and allot resources appropriately. This strategy acts as a road map to direct their marketing initiatives and guarantee a methodical approach to reader outreach.

Use Scheduling and Productivity Tools: To effectively organize their promotional activities, judging authors use scheduling and productivity tools. For organization and project management purposes, they employ calendars, task managers, or project management software. Authors may consistently interact with their audience and keep up a consistent presence by exercising self-control and sticking to a timetable.

Encourage Testimonials and Endorsements: Marketing strategies that are judge-oriented actively seek out recommendations and reviews from notable people or happy customers. The book's quality is attested to by industry experts, well-known individuals, or reputable professionals who will also promote it to their own networks or following. These recommendations help establish trustworthiness and act as potent social proof.

Establish Partnerships and Collaborations: Judging authors look to form alliances and work together with influential people, organizations, or other authors who write in the same genre. They collaborate to promote each other's publications or events by taking advantage of their shared audiences. Authors can increase their exposure and reach by carefully partnering with like-minded people or organizations.

Organize targeted marketing campaigns: Advertising campaigns that are properly thought out and targeted are used in judging-oriented strategies. Where their intended audience is most likely to be present, major platforms, magazines, or internet channels are identified by authors. They create engaging ad copy, choose pertinent keywords, and apply data-driven tactics to increase the effectiveness of their advertising campaigns.

Monitor and Analyze Marketing Analytics: In order to gauge the success of their initiatives, judging authors assiduously track and evaluate marketing analytics. To gauge the efficacy of their marketing initiatives, they monitor information like website traffic, click-through rates, conversion rates, and engagement indicators. Judging authors pinpoint areas for development, make informed decisions, and modify their marketing strategy by examining these indicators.

The focus of Judging Book Marketing Tactics is mostly on strategic preparation, coordination, and methodical implementation. Authors can effectively position their books and raise their visibility among their target audience by developing well-structured marketing plans, leveraging productivity tools, obtaining endorsements, and running focused advertising campaigns. Judging methods' methodical and focused approach makes sure that marketing initiatives are well-coordinated and in line with the general goals of the book.

Chapter Ten

Perceiving (P) Book Marketing Tactics

When promoting a book, perception (P) book marketing tactics and techniques call for spontaneity, adaptability, and flexibility. They place a high value on remaining open to new possibilities, trying out different approaches, and quickly reacting to market changes. Here are a few illustrations of perceptions of book marketing strategies:

Accept Flexibility in Marketing Strategy: Authors who are perceiving-oriented are open to experimenting with various marketing techniques and adapting their approach in response to comments and responses. They are open to experimenting with novel approaches, changing their messaging, and using various platforms for advertising. They can adjust to shifting market conditions and capture unanticipated opportunities thanks to their flexibility.

Engage in Spontaneous Interactions: Perceiving authors welcome sudden interactions with readers and future fans. They engage in conversations as they develop, respond to comments, and actively participate in social media discussions. Authors can create organic connections and cultivate a devoted following by being in the moment and showing real interest in their audience.

Use social listening tools to identify market trends: Utilizing social listening technologies to keep tabs on conversations, trends, and discussions pertinent to their book or target audience is a component of perception-oriented techniques. This includes researching the subjects that readers find interesting, learning about new developments in their field, or having conversations about the themes of their books are all topics that perceiving authors pay attention to. These authors are more inclined to adapt their material and messaging to fit with readers' current interests by making use of real-time information.

Utilize User-Generated Content: As part of their marketing plan, perceptive authors promote and make use of user-generated content. They invite readers to share their thoughts, produce fan art, submit reviews, and surveys, or take part in competitions centered around the book. Perceiving authors can tap into the enthusiasm and ingenuity of their readership by exhibiting and promoting user-generated content, which creates buzz and fosters a sense of community.

Participate in Unexpected Events and Possibilities: Taking advantage of unplanned opportunities that fit the book's themes or target audience are examples of perceiving-oriented approaches. This includes but is not limited to taking part in virtual events or panels, writing guest articles for related blogs or websites, or participating in online book discussions. Perceiving Authors can increase their audience and attract new readers by being receptive to new opportunities.

Stress Personal Authenticity: Perceiving authors place a strong emphasis on being true to themselves and being authentic in their marketing endeavors. They divulge private information, opinions, or sneak peeks into their writing process. Perceiving authors draw readers by highlighting their distinctive viewpoint and voice, who value their genuineness and relate to their personal writing journey.

Overall, Perceiving Book Marketing Tactics emphasize flexibility, impulsiveness, and responsiveness. Perceiving Authors can establish a true and dynamic connection with their audience by embracing flexibility, participating in impromptu events, exploiting user-generated material, utilizing social listening tools, and emphasizing personal authenticity. With Perceiving methods, authors can navigate the always-shifting world of book promotion and take advantage of opportunities as they present themselves.

Chapter Eleven

Book Marketing tactics for your specific temperament.

N ow as promised we get to what I hope will be the juiciest part of the book for you: An individualized promotion plan based on YOUR unique temperament type. In the following pages, you will find specific suggested tactics that align with your individual temperament. Find which ones resonate with you and use them to the hilt. Also, I'd encourage you to consider additional tactics to your promotional repertoire. Remember the tactics suggested are not meant to be limiting but a primer to jumpstart you on developing a possible plan that naturally resonates with you. Always feel free to explore and use any and all tactics that will help you achieve your promotional goals. Also, take a look at those temperaments that are adjacent to you as they also may have tactics that speak to you. Now let's dive in!

ISTJ (Introverted, Sensing, Thinking, Judging)

ISTJ (Introverted, Sensing, Thinking, and Judging) individuals are known for their practicality, attention to detail, and reliability. When it comes to promoting their books, and possess a variety of ways to leverage that strength:

Focus on a targeted audience: ISTJs excel at understanding and catering to specific audience needs. They should identify their niche market and tailor their marketing efforts accordingly. By focusing on a specific audience, they can create targeted messages and content that resonate with their readers.

Utilize traditional marketing channels: ISTJs often appreciate traditional methods and prefer tried-and-true strategies. They can leverage channels like radio, TV, and traditional newspapers to reach their audience. Placing ads, participating in interviews, or writing articles for print media can help them gain visibility among their target readers.

Create a professional online presence: While ISTJs may lean toward offline methods, having a strong online presence is essential in today's digital world. They can build a professional website and maintain active profiles on platforms like LinkedIn and Goodreads. Focus on presenting their credentials, showcasing their book's value, and providing a clear call to action.

Leverage email marketing: ISTJs value efficiency and practicality, making email marketing a suitable strategy for them. They can build an email list of interested readers and send targeted messages about their book releases, updates, and exclusive offers. Providing valuable content and personalized recommendations can engage their audience effectively.

Seek endorsements and reviews: ISTJs value credibility and reliability. They can reach out to well-known authors, industry experts, or influencers in their genre to seek endorsements or reviews. Positive feedback and recommendations from trusted sources can significantly boost their book's reputation and attract new readers.

Utilize book signing events: While introverted, ISTJs can still benefit from in-person interactions. They can arrange book signing events at local bookstores, libraries, or literary festivals. By connecting directly with readers, they can build relationships, answer questions, and create a personal connection that resonates with their audience.

Provide informative content: ISTJs' preference for facts and practicality can be harnessed through informative content. They can write blog posts, and articles, or create videos that provide valuable insights, practical tips, or in-depth knowledge related to their book's subject matter. Sharing their expertise can position them as authoritative figures and attract readers interested in their niche.

Collaborate with book clubs or reading groups: ISTJs can approach local book clubs or online reading groups to collaborate. They can offer author Q&A sessions, discussion guides, or exclusive content to enhance the reading experience for members. Building relationships with book enthusiasts can lead to word-of-mouth recommendations and expand their readership.

Utilize social media selectively: While ISTJs may not be naturally drawn to extensive social media engagement; they can still utilize selective platforms that align with their target audience. They can choose platforms like LinkedIn or niche-specific forums where they can engage in meaningful discussions, share valuable content, and connect with potential readers in a focused manner.

Provide structured promotions and discounts: ISTJs appreciate structure and order. They can offer limited-time promotions, bundle deals, or discounts with clear start and end dates. By providing a clear framework, ISTJs can attract readers who appreciate straightforward offers and take prompt action.

In summary, ISTJs can leverage their practicality, attention to detail, and reliability to promote their books effectively. By focusing on targeted marketing, utilizing traditional and online channels selectively, and providing valuable content, they can engage their audience and build a strong reputation as dependable authors.

The following promotional activities tend to ISTJ's strengths.

- Develop a Professional Book Cover

- Offer Signed Copies or Personalized Bookplates

- Participate in Local Book Signings

- Collaborate with Local Bookstores

- Seek Speaking Engagements at Conferences

- Develop a Comprehensive Book Marketing Plan

ISFJ (Introverted, Sensing, Feeling, Judging):

ISFJ (Introverted, Sensing, Feeling, Judging) individuals are known for their compassion, practicality, and attention to detail. When it comes to promoting their books, they can leverage their strengths in the following ways:

Cultivate personal connections: ISFJs excel at building meaningful relationships. They can focus on establishing personal connections with readers, book clubs, and influencers in their genre. Engaging in conversations, responding to comments and messages, and showing genuine interest in their audience can help them create a loyal and supportive community.

Leverage word-of-mouth marketing: ISFJs are trusted and dependable individuals. They can encourage their readers to share their book with others through word-of-mouth marketing. Providing exceptional reader experiences, engaging in genuine conversations, and offering personalized recommendations can help generate positive buzz and organic referrals.

Engage in social media platforms: While introverted, ISFJs can utilize social media platforms to connect with their audience. They can focus on platforms like Instagram, Facebook, or Twitter to share updates about their book, behind-the-scenes insights, and meaningful stories. Engaging with followers through comments, direct messages, and personalized interactions can create a sense of community and foster reader loyalty.

Create visually appealing content: ISFJs have an eye for detail and aesthetics. They can create visually appealing content, such as graphics, quote images, or book-related photos, to engage their audience. Captivating visuals can help create an emotional connection with readers and draw them in to learn more about the book.

Seek book reviews and testimonials: ISFJs value authentic feedback and personal experiences. They can reach out to book bloggers, reviewers, and early readers to request honest reviews and testimonials. Sharing positive reviews on their website, social media platforms and promotional materials can build trust and credibility among potential readers.

Participate in book-related events: ISFJs can benefit from participating in book-related events such as literary festivals, book signings, or author panels. These events provide opportunities to connect with readers, network with fellow authors, and share their passion for writing. Personal interactions at events can leave a lasting impression on attendees.

Collaborate with book clubs and reading communities: ISFJs can engage with book clubs and reading communities to foster discussions around their book. They can offer to join virtual or in-person book club meetings, provide discussion guides, or answer readers' questions. Collaborating with these groups can create a sense of community and generate valuable feedback.

Utilize email newsletters: ISFJs can leverage email newsletters to communicate directly with their audience. They can provide regular updates about their book, share exclusive content, and offer special promotions to subscribers. By cultivating a dedicated email list, they can establish a more intimate and personal connection with their readers.

Focus on emotional storytelling: ISFJs are in tune with their emotions and the emotions of others. They can leverage this strength by focusing on emotional storytelling in their book promotion. Sharing personal anecdotes, heartfelt messages, or stories behind their writing process can resonate deeply with readers who value emotional connections.

Seek support from local communities: ISFJs often have strong ties to their local communities. They can leverage these connections by reaching out to local bookstores, libraries, or community organizations for book signings, speaking engagements, or collaborative events. Engaging with the local community can create a strong support system and generate local buzz for their book.

In summary, ISFJs can promote their books effectively by leveraging their compassion, attention to detail, and personal connections. By engaging in genuine interactions, utilizing social media platforms, and focusing on emotional storytelling, they can create a loyal reader base and establish a meaningful presence in the literary community.

The following promotional activities tend to ISFJ's strengths.

- Participate in Book Fairs and Literary Events

- Create a Captivating Author Bio and Book Description

- Establish Partnerships with Non-profit Organizations

- Attend Local Book Signings or Author Meet-and-Greets

- Utilize Targeted Online Advertising Platforms

- Collaborate with Book Clubs or Reading Subscription Services

INFJ (Introverted, Intuitive, Feeling, Judging):

INFJ (Introverted, Intuitive, Feeling, Judging) individuals are known for their empathy, creativity, and idealism. When it comes to promoting their books, they can leverage their strengths in the following ways:

Connect on an emotional level: INFJs excel at understanding and connecting with people's emotions. They can promote their books by appealing to readers' emotions and values. Creating heartfelt and authentic messages that resonate with the deeper aspects of human experience can draw readers in and establish a strong emotional connection.

Utilize content marketing: INFJs can leverage their creativity and intuitive insights through content marketing. They can write thought-provoking blog posts, and articles, or create engaging videos that align with the themes of their book. Sharing valuable content that sparks meaningful conversations can attract readers who resonate with their ideas.

Engage with book clubs and online communities: INFJs can actively participate in book clubs, online forums, and social media groups related to their book's genre. Engaging in discussions, answering questions, and sharing insights can create a sense of community and generate interest in their work. Building relationships with like-minded readers can result in loyal fans and advocates.

Leverage social media platforms: While introverted, INFJs can utilize social media platforms to share their book and connect with readers. They can focus on platforms like Instagram, Twitter, or Tumblr where they can showcase their creativity through visually appealing posts or share profound insights that resonate with their audience. Authentic engagement and meaningful interactions can foster a dedicated following.

Seek opportunities for public speaking: INFJs can leverage their ability to inspire and communicate effectively by seeking opportunities for public speaking engagements. They can participate in literary events, conferences, or TEDx talks to share their knowledge, experiences, and passion for their book's subject matter. Engaging with live audiences can create a lasting impact and generate interest in their work.

Collaborate with influencers and bloggers: INFJs can collaborate with influencers, bloggers, and podcasters who align with their book's themes and target audience. Partnering with influential individuals can expand their reach and expose their books to new readers. Guest blogging, interviews, or joint creative projects can create mutual benefits and generate buzz.

Utilize email newsletters: INFJs can cultivate a loyal readership by utilizing email newsletters. They can provide exclusive content, behind-the-scenes insights, and updates about their book's progress. INFJs can infuse their newsletters with their unique writing style, offering a personal touch that resonates with their readers and builds a sense of connection and anticipation.

Engage in book signings and author events: INFJs can host book signings, author readings, or workshops to engage directly with readers. These events provide an opportunity to connect on a personal level, share their passion for their book, and forge genuine connections with their audience. Building personal relationships can lead to long-term support and word-of-mouth recommendations.

Seek book endorsements and reviews: INFJs can reach out to influential authors, experts, or respected figures in their field to request endorsements or reviews for their books. Positive testimonials can enhance their book's credibility and attract readers who value the recommendations of trusted sources. Reviews on platforms like Goodreads or Amazon can also contribute to visibility and discoverability.

Support a cause or charitable initiative: INFJs' idealistic nature often aligns with a desire to make a positive impact. They can promote their book by connecting it with a cause or charitable initiative that resonates with their themes. Donating a portion of book sales or organizing fundraising events can not only raise awareness but also attract readers who share their values.

In summary, INFJs can promote their books effectively by leveraging their empathy, creativity, and idealism. By connecting on an emotional level, utilizing content marketing, and actively engaging

The following promotional activities tend to INFJ's strengths.

- Seek Endorsements from Well-known Authors or Experts

- Organize Blog Tours or Virtual Author Interviews

- Write Guest Articles for Relevant Publications

- Host Virtual Book Club Discussions or Author Q&A Sessions

- Develop an Author Newsletter

- Collaborate with Book Reviewers or Booktubers for Video Reviews

- Participating in Book-related Podcast Interviews

INTJ (Introverted, Intuitive, Thinking, Judging):

INTJ (Introverted, Intuitive, Thinking, Judging) individuals are known for their logical thinking, strategic approach, and independent nature. When it comes to promoting their books, they can leverage their strengths in the following ways:

Develop a targeted marketing strategy: INTJs excel at strategic planning. They should develop a comprehensive marketing strategy that aligns with their book's target audience and goals. By conducting market research, identifying key demographics, and defining their unique selling points, they can create targeted messages and tailor their marketing efforts accordingly.

Utilize digital marketing channels: INTJs can effectively leverage digital marketing channels to reach their audience. They can focus on strategies such as search engine optimization (SEO) to increase online visibility, content marketing to provide valuable insights related to their book's topic, and pay-per-click advertising to target specific keywords and demographics.

Create an authoritative online presence: INTJs can establish themselves as experts in their field by creating a professional and authoritative online presence. This can include building a well-designed website, maintaining active profiles on professional networks like LinkedIn, and regularly sharing valuable and thought-provoking content that showcases their knowledge and expertise.

Write informative blog posts and articles: INTJs' logical and analytical thinking can be channeled into writing informative blog posts and articles related to their book's subject matter. By sharing valuable insights, tips, and practical advice, they can attract readers who are interested in their niche and position themselves as authorities in the field.

Engage in thought leadership: INTJs can leverage their logical thinking and unique perspectives to engage in thought leadership. They can contribute articles to industry publications, participate in panel discussions or podcast interviews, and share their expertise on relevant platforms. By offering valuable insights and challenging conventional thinking, they can attract a dedicated following and generate interest in their book.

Leverage social media for targeted engagement: While introverted, INTJs can utilize social media strategically. They can select platforms that align with their book's target audience, such as LinkedIn or Twitter, and engage in meaningful discussions and thought-provoking conversations. By providing insightful comments, sharing valuable content, and connecting with industry influencers, they can expand their network and reach.

Seek endorsements from respected figures: INTJs can leverage their logical and strategic thinking to identify respected figures within their industry or niche. By reaching out to these individuals and requesting endorsements or testimonials for their books, they can enhance their credibility and attract readers who value the recommendations of trusted authorities.

Participate in speaking engagements and conferences: INTJs can showcase their expertise by participating in speaking engagements and conferences. They can present on topics related to their book, offer workshops, or engage in panel discussions. By sharing their knowledge and unique perspectives, they can establish themselves as industry thought leaders and attract attention to their book.

Utilize targeted advertising campaigns: INTJs can employ data-driven advertising campaigns to reach their specific target audience. By utilizing platforms like Google Ads or Facebook Ads, they can strategically select keywords, demographics, and interests that align with their book's themes. This approach allows them to reach potential readers who are more likely to be interested in their book.

Leverage email marketing for direct communication: INTJs can utilize email marketing to establish direct communication with their audience. By building an email list of interested readers, they can send regular newsletters with updates, exclusive content, and personalized recommendations. This direct communication allows them to cultivate a loyal reader base and keep their audience engaged.

In summary, INTJs can promote their books effectively by leveraging their logical thinking, strategic approach, and independent nature. By developing a targeted marketing strategy, utilizing digital channels, creating an authoritative online presence, and engaging in thought leadership, they can attract readers who value their expertise and analytical insights.

The following promotional activities tend to INTJ's strengths.

- Conduct Market Research to Identify Target Audience

- Create an Author Website or Blog

- Run a Pre-launch Campaign to Generate Buzz

- Offer Advanced Reader Copies (ARCs) for Reviews

- Utilize Search Engine Optimization (SEO) Techniques

- Utilize Online Advertising Platforms like Google Ads or Amazon Ads

- Offer Special Editions with Bonus Content or Additional Chapters

ISTP (Introverted, Sensing, Thinking, Perceiving):

ISTP (Introverted, Sensing, Thinking, Perceiving) individuals are known for their practicality, adaptability, and hands-on approach. When it comes to promoting their books, they can leverage their strengths in the following ways:

Utilize visual content: ISTPs can make use of visual content to engage their audience. They can create visually appealing graphics, videos, or infographics related to their book's themes. Visual content can capture attention and communicate information in a concise and engaging manner, attracting readers who appreciate a practical and visually stimulating approach.

Engage in experiential marketing: ISTPs can showcase their book through experiential marketing tactics. They can organize book launch events, interactive workshops, or demonstrations related to their book's subject matter. These hands-on experiences can provide a tangible connection to their work and generate interest among readers who prefer a more interactive and immersive approach.

Leverage their technical expertise: ISTPs are often skilled in technical areas. They can utilize their expertise to create instructional or practical content that demonstrates their knowledge. This can include creating tutorial videos, writing informative blog posts, or offering practical tips and tricks related to their book's topic. By showcasing their technical proficiency, they can attract readers who value practical advice and insights.

Engage in niche communities and forums: ISTPs can actively participate in online forums, social media groups, or niche communities related to their book's subject matter. They can share their expertise, answer questions, and contribute to discussions. By being a valuable and knowledgeable presence in these communities, they can build credibility and attract readers who are actively seeking information on their book's topic.

Utilize search engine optimization (SEO): ISTPs can leverage their practicality by focusing on search engine optimization (SEO) techniques. By conducting keyword research and optimizing their website or blog content, they can increase their visibility in search engine results. This can help potential readers find their book when searching for relevant topics or keywords.

Offer practical case studies or real-life examples: ISTPs can provide practical case studies or real-life examples that demonstrate the value and application of their book's concepts. This can be done through blog posts, guest articles, or even short videos. By illustrating how their ideas or methods have worked in real-world scenarios, they can build credibility and attract readers who are looking for practical solutions.

Collaborate with influencers or experts: ISTPs can collaborate with influencers or experts in their book's niche to expand their reach and credibility. By partnering with individuals who have a strong following or established expertise, they can tap into their audience and gain exposure. This can include joint promotions, guest blogging, or participating in collaborative projects.

Utilize email marketing for targeted communication: ISTPs can utilize email marketing to directly communicate with their audience. By building an email list and sending targeted newsletters or updates, they can share valuable content, announce book-related events, and offer exclusive discounts or bonuses. This direct communication allows them to connect with interested readers who appreciate practical and relevant information.

Participate in industry events and trade shows: ISTPs can take advantage of industry events, trade shows, or conferences related to their book's subject matter. They can participate as speakers, panelists, or exhibitors to showcase their expertise and engage with a targeted audience. Networking with professionals in their field can lead to valuable connections and potential collaborations.

Leverage video content and tutorials: ISTPs can create video content, tutorials, or demonstrations that provide practical insights and guidance related to their book's topic. Videos can be shared on platforms like YouTube or social media, providing a visual and hands-on experience for viewers. This can attract readers who prefer interactive and visually engaging content.

The following promotional activities tend to ISTP strengths.
- Develop Partnerships with Independent Bookstores

- Network with Authors and Industry Professionals

- Participate in Podcast Interviews

- Create Book Trailers or Promotional Videos

- Engage with Book Review Bloggers

- Collaborate with Influencers or Bookstagrammers

- Seek Opportunities for Cross-promotion with Other Authors

ISFP (Introverted, Sensing, Feeling, Perceiving)

ISFP (Introverted, Sensing, Feeling, Perceiving) individuals are known for their creativity, sensitivity, and appreciation for aesthetics. When it comes to promoting their books, they can leverage their strengths in the following ways:

Emphasize personal connection: ISFPs can connect with their audience on a personal and emotional level. They can share their own stories, experiences, and emotions related to their book's themes. By being authentic and vulnerable, they can create a genuine connection with readers who resonate with their feelings and values.

Utilize visually appealing aesthetics: ISFPs have an eye for aesthetics and can create visually captivating promotional materials. They can design beautiful book covers, graphics, or social media posts that reflect the mood and tone of their book. Visual appeal can attract readers who appreciate artistic expression and are drawn to visually stunning content.

Engage in artistic collaborations: ISFPs can collaborate with other artists, such as illustrators, photographers, or designers, to create unique and visually striking promotional materials. By combining their creative talents with others, they can create a synergy that enhances the overall promotional impact. This can include creating joint art exhibitions, co-authoring projects, or collaborating on visually appealing book trailers.

Share behind-the-scenes content: ISFPs can provide glimpses into their creative process and share behind-the-scenes content with their audience. This can include sharing sketches, drafts, or insights into their inspirations and artistic choices. By offering this inside perspective, they can engage readers who appreciate the creative journey and the personal touch behind their work.

Utilize storytelling techniques: ISFPs can leverage their storytelling abilities to create engaging promotional content. They can craft compelling narratives that evoke emotions and captivate their audience. This can be done through blog posts, social media updates, or video content that shares snippets of their book's story or themes. By tapping into the power of storytelling, they can attract readers who value meaningful narratives.

Participate in book clubs and reading communities: ISFPs can actively engage with book clubs, online reading communities, or forums that align with their book's genre or themes. By participating in discussions, sharing their insights, and connecting with readers who appreciate their artistic perspective, they can build a dedicated following and generate word-of-mouth recommendations.

Leverage social media platforms focused on visual content: ISFPs can make use of social media platforms that prioritize visual content, such as Instagram or Pinterest. They can showcase their book, share aesthetically pleasing images, and curate a visually appealing feed that aligns with their book's style and themes. By leveraging these platforms, they can attract readers who appreciate artistry and creative expression.

Host book launch events with an artistic flair: ISFPs can organize book launch events that incorporate artistic elements. This can include live music performances, art exhibitions, or interactive installations that reflect the essence of their book. By creating a multisensory experience, they can engage attendees on an emotional and artistic level.

Collaborate with influencers in creative fields: ISFPs can collaborate with influencers, bloggers, or content creators who have a strong presence in creative fields. By partnering with individuals who share a similar artistic aesthetic or audience, they can tap into their followers and expand their reach. This can include joint promotions, creative collaborations, or featured guest posts.

Leverage book review platforms focused on literary analysis: ISFPs can target book review platforms or blogs that emphasize literary analysis, symbolism, and the emotional impact of literature. They can send review copies to these platforms and engage with reviewers who appreciate their artistic approach. Positive reviews from these platforms can attract readers who value deep insights and introspective reading experiences.

Offer limited-edition or artistically designed book editions: ISFPs can create special editions of their books that appeal to collectors and fans of artistic artisanship. These editions can feature unique cover designs, special illustrations, or additional artistic elements. By offering something visually distinctive and exclusive, they can attract readers who appreciate the artistic value and collectible nature of books.

Engage in experiential marketing: ISFPs can create immersive and experiential marketing campaigns that resonate with their audience. This can involve organizing book-related events, such as poetry readings, art showcases, or interactive workshops. By providing an experiential journey that connects with their book's themes, they can leave a lasting impression and build a dedicated following.

Leverage the power of testimonials and personal recommendations: ISFPs can encourage readers to share their personal experiences and recommendations about their book. They can collect testimonials, create quote graphics, or feature reader stories on their website or social media platforms. Authentic and heartfelt recommendations can have a powerful impact on attracting readers who value personal connections and recommendations from like-minded individuals.

Collaborate with booktubers or bookstagrammers: ISFPs can reach out to popular booktubers (YouTube channels focused on books) or bookstagrammers (Instagram accounts dedicated to books) whose aesthetics and values align with their book. By sending them review-copies or collaborating on book-related content, they can tap into their followers' enthusiasm and expand their reach among readers who appreciate visually appealing books.

Leverage the power of book trailers and visual storytelling: ISFPs can create captivating book trailers that visually convey the essence of their story. By incorporating artistic elements, music, and evocative visuals, they can capture the interest of potential readers and ignite their curiosity. Visual storytelling can create an emotional connection and inspire readers to delve into their book.

Participate in literary festivals and artistic events: ISFPs can participate in literary festivals, art exhibitions, or events that celebrate creativity and artistic expression. By showcasing their book in these environments, they can engage with a diverse audience of art enthusiasts, fellow authors, and readers who appreciate the intersection of literature and the arts.

Foster relationships with local independent bookstores: ISFPs can build relationships with local independent bookstores that align with their artistic sensibilities. They can organize book signings, author talks, or collaborate on special events. Independent bookstores often have a dedicated community of readers who value unique and thoughtfully curated books, providing a fantastic opportunity for connection and promotion.

Create a visually appealing author website or blog: ISFPs can establish an online presence through a visually appealing author website or blog. They can showcase their artwork, share their creative process, and provide behind-the-scenes glimpses of their book. By creating a visually captivating online platform, they can attract readers who are drawn to their artistic style and storytelling approach.

Engage in email marketing with a personal touch: ISFPs can utilize email marketing to communicate directly with their audience. By sending personalized newsletters, updates, or bonus content, they can foster a sense of connection and exclusivity. Email marketing allows them to maintain ongoing communication and build a loyal community of readers who appreciate their artistic vision.

Leverage the power of word-of-mouth marketing: ISFPs can actively engage with their readers, respond to their messages and comments, and cultivate a sense of community around their books. By nurturing authentic relationships with their readers and encouraging them to share their love for the book with others, they can harness the power of word-of-mouth marketing, which is particularly influential for readers seeking unique and emotionally resonant literature.

In summary, ISFPs can promote their books effectively by leveraging their creativity, sensitivity, and appreciation for aesthetics. By emphasizing personal connections, utilizing visually appealing aesthetics, and engaging in artistic collaborations, they can attract readers who value artistic expression and emotional resonance. They can also leverage social media platforms focused on visual content, participate in book clubs and reading communities, and collaborate with influencers in creative fields to expand their reach. Additionally, they can host book launch events with an artistic flair, offer limited-edition or artistically designed book editions, and engage in experiential marketing to create immersive experiences for their audience. By fostering relationships with local independent bookstores, creating visually appealing author websites or blogs, and utilizing email marketing with a personal touch, they can connect with their readers on a deeper level. Lastly, by leveraging the power of testimonials, participating in literary festivals and artistic events, and encouraging word-of-mouth marketing, they can build a loyal community of readers who appreciate their unique artistic perspective.

Remember, each author's journey and promotional strategy may differ based on their individual style and target audience. It's important for ISFPs to tap into their creativity, authenticity, and passion for their work to effectively promote their books and connect with readers who appreciate their artistic vision.

The following promotional activities tend to ISFP (Introverted, Sensing, Feeling, Perceiving) strengths

- Collaborate with Book Clubs for Reading and Discussion Sessions

- Offer Exclusive Bonus Content or Additional Resources

- Participate in Genre-specific Conventions or Trade Shows

- Create Visually Appealing Book Quote Graphics

- Collaborate with Book Influencers on YouTube or Video Platforms

- Run Social Media Contests or Giveaways

- Create a Book-themed Merchandise Line

INFP (Introverted, Intuitive, Feeling, Perceiving)

INFP (Introverted, Intuitive, Feeling, Perceiving) individuals are known for their deep introspection, empathy, and creative expression. When it comes to promoting their books, they can leverage their strengths in the following ways:

Tap into their authentic voice: INFPs can promote their books by staying true to their unique perspective and writing style. They can convey their authentic voice through their marketing materials, such as website content, social media posts, and author bios. By expressing their genuine thoughts and emotions, they can attract readers who resonate with their sincerity and heartfelt storytelling.

Utilize storytelling and emotional connection: INFPs can create promotional content that centers around storytelling and evoking emotions. They can share personal anecdotes, emotional insights, and thought-provoking narratives related to their book's themes. By connecting with readers on an emotional level, they can generate curiosity and engagement.

Engage in personal interactions: INFPs can engage with their readers through personal interactions, such as responding to emails, comments, and messages on social media. By actively listening to their readers and fostering meaningful conversations, they can build a loyal community of supporters who appreciate their work and feel a personal connection.

Create visually appealing and inspiring content: INFPs can leverage their creative abilities to design visually appealing and inspiring content that reflects the essence of their book. This can include creating aesthetically pleasing graphics, mood boards, or book trailers. By incorporating their artistic sensibilities, they can captivate the attention of potential readers who appreciate beauty and creative expression.

Participate in online communities and forums: INFPs can actively participate in online communities, forums, or social media groups that align with their book's genre or themes. By contributing thoughtful insights, sharing book recommendations, and engaging in discussions, they can establish themselves as knowledgeable and passionate contributors. This can help them build credibility and attract readers who value their unique perspective.

Leverage the power of book blogging and reviews: INFPs can reach out to book bloggers and reviewers who specialize in their book's genre. By providing review copies and engaging in honest and respectful conversations, they can generate buzz and positive word-of-mouth recommendations. INFPs can also consider starting their own book blog to share their thoughts on books, connect with like-minded readers, and create a supportive network.

Host virtual events and author Q&A sessions: INFPs can host virtual events, such as online book launches, author Q&A sessions, or live readings. These events provide an opportunity for readers to engage directly with the author and gain insights into their creative process and inspirations. By creating a sense of intimacy and accessibility, INFPs can connect deeply with their readers.

Share behind-the-scenes content and writing updates: INFPs can offer glimpses into their writing process, including sharing writing updates, excerpts, and be-hind-the-scenes content. This can be done through blog posts, social media updates, or newsletters. By involving their readers in their creative journey, they can create a sense of anticipation and foster a loyal following.

Collaborate with other creatives: INFPs can collaborate with artists, musicians, or photographers to create multimedia projects that complement their books. By combining different artistic mediums, they can reach a wider audience and create a unique promo-tional experience. This can involve creating book-inspired artwork, collaborating on a book soundtrack, or featuring photography that captures the essence of their book.

Leverage the power of social media and online platforms: INFPs can leverage social media platforms, such as Instagram, Twitter, or Tumblr, to share their thoughts, inspiration, and snippets of their book. They can curate a visually cohesive and inspiring feed that resonates with their target audience. INFPs can also consider.

Engage in guest blogging: INFPs can write guest blog posts for websites or platforms that align with their book's genre or target audience. This allows them to showcase their writing skills, share their unique insights, and reach a wider readership.

Offer free or discounted promotions: INFPs can periodically offer their book for free or at discounted prices to attract new readers and generate buzz. This can be done through platforms like Amazon Kindle Direct Publishing (KDP) Select, where authors can run limited-time promotions to reach a larger audience.

Participate in book clubs and reading groups: INFPs can actively engage in book clubs and reading groups to connect with readers who share similar interests. They can join online book clubs or local meetups to discuss their book or participate in reading challenges. By fostering meaningful discussions, they can create a sense of community and build a dedicated readership.

Utilize email marketing with a personal touch: INFPs can establish a newsletter or email list to communicate directly with their readers. They can share updates about their writing journey, exclusive content, and insights into their upcoming projects. By nurturing personal connections through email, they can build a loyal fan base that eagerly awaits their next book.

Offer pre-order incentives: INFPs can create incentives for readers to pre-order their books, such as exclusive bonus content, signed copies, or personalized thank-you notes. This can help generate early interest and build anticipation around their book release.

Collaborate with booktubers and bookstagrammers: INFPs can collaborate with popular booktubers (YouTube channels focused on books) and bookstagrammers (Instagram accounts dedicated to books) to gain exposure among their followers. They can send review copies, participate in author interviews, or organize joint giveaways to reach a broader audience that appreciates book-related content.

Leverage crowdfunding platforms: INFPs can consider crowdfunding platforms like Kickstarter or Indiegogo to fund their book projects and generate pre-orders. By offering unique rewards or limited-edition perks to backers, they can engage their audience and build a community of dedicated supporters.

Host writing workshops or webinars: INFPs can leverage their writing skills and insights to host writing workshops or webinars. They can share their knowledge on topics like character development, world-building, or the creative process. By positioning themselves as knowledgeable and supportive mentors, they can attract aspiring writers who may also become interested in their books.

Network with other authors and industry professionals: INFPs can actively network with other authors, editors, publishers, and literary agents through writing conferences, online forums, or social media groups. Building connections within the publishing industry can open doors to collaborative opportunities, promotional partnerships, and valuable insights.

Be active in online book communities: INFPs can participate in online book communities like Goodreads, Reddit's book-related subreddits, or niche forums. By contributing book reviews, and recommendations, and engaging in discussions, they can establish their presence and connect with enthusiastic readers who might be interested in their work.

Remember, these are general suggestions, and it's essential for INFP authors to personalize their promotional strategies based on their specific book, target audience, and comfort level. By staying true to their authentic voice and leveraging their innate creativity and empathy, INFPs can effectively promote their books and connect with readers who appreciate their heartfelt and introspective storytelling.

The following promotional activities tend to INFP (Introverted, Intuitive, Feeling, Perceiving) strengths.

- Create a Compelling Book with a Unique Concept

- Host Virtual Book Tours with Multiple Stops

- Develop Partnerships with Book Bloggers

- Write Guest Articles for Online Magazines or Websites

- Participate in Online Book Communities or Forums

- Run a Social Media Campaign to Generate Buzz

- Participate in Book-related Hashtag Challenges or Trends

INTP (Introverted, Intuitive, Thinking, Perceiving)

INTP (Introverted, Intuitive, Thinking, Perceiving) individuals are known for their intellectual curiosity, analytical thinking, and love for exploring ideas. When it comes to promoting their books, they can leverage their strengths in the following ways:

Showcase your expertise and unique insights: INTPs can promote their books by emphasizing their expertise in a specific subject or their ability to offer unique insights. They can highlight the depth of research, innovative ideas, and thought-provoking concepts present in their work. By positioning themselves as intellectual authorities, they can attract readers who value intellectual stimulation and seek knowledge.

Engage in intellectual discussions: INTPs can engage in intellectual discussions related to their book's themes or genre. They can participate in online forums, discussion groups, or platforms like Quora and Reddit to share their perspectives, provide valuable insights, and contribute to meaningful conversations. By showcasing their intellectual prowess, they can pique the interest of like-minded readers and potential fans.

Utilize blogging and long-form content: INTPs can excel in creating detailed and analytical content through blogging or writing articles related to their book's subject matter. By sharing in-depth analyses, thought experiments, or theories on their blog or guest posting on relevant platforms, they can establish their credibility and attract readers who appreciate their intellectual approach.

Leverage social media for sharing ideas: INTPs can utilize social media platforms like Twitter, LinkedIn, or Medium to share their thoughts, ideas, and excerpts from their book. They can engage in conversations with followers, share interesting articles or research findings, and showcase their intellectual interests. By fostering a community of intellectually curious individuals, they can create a supportive network of readers.

Offer free resources or samples: INTPs can provide free resources, such as e-books, white papers, or sample chapters, which offer a glimpse into their book's content and demonstrate their expertise. This can help build credibility, generate interest, and encourage readers to explore their full work.

Participate in speaking engagements or podcasts: INTPs can showcase their expertise and promote their books by participating in speaking engagements, panel discussions, or podcasts. They can share their ideas, insights, and research findings with a broader audience. By presenting their work in a structured and intellectual manner, they can capture the attention of listeners who appreciate intellectual discourse.

Collaborate with influencers and experts: INTPs can collaborate with influencers, experts, or academics in their field to gain exposure and credibility. They can co-author articles, participate in joint projects, or engage in interviews or roundtable discussions. By associating themselves with respected individuals, they can expand their reach and tap into their partner's existing audience.

Create informative videos or webinars: INTPs can leverage their ability to present complex ideas in a clear and concise manner by creating informative videos or hosting webinars. They can break down complex concepts from their book, provide explanations, and engage with their audience in real-time. By offering valuable educational content, they can attract viewers who appreciate intellectual stimulation.

Provide expert opinions and commentary: INTPs can position themselves as experts within their field by providing expert opinions or commentary on relevant topics. They can contribute articles to publications, offer insights through media interviews, or share their thoughts through guest blog posts. By demonstrating their expertise beyond their book, they can build a reputation as a respected authority.

Foster relationships with book clubs and academic institutions: INTPs can reach out to book clubs, academic institutions, or intellectual communities to discuss their book or offer to facilitate discussions. By engaging with groups that value intellectual exploration, they can spark interest, generate book recommendations, and establish connections with readers who appreciate their intellectual pursuits.

Remember, these suggestions are meant to serve as a starting point, and INTP authors should tailor their marketing approaches based on their specific book, target audience, and personal preferences. By embracing their unique strengths as analytical thinkers and intellectual explorers, INTPs can effectively promote their books and connect with readers who appreciate their intellectual pursuits.

The following promotional activities tend to INTP (Introverted, Intuitive, Thinking, Perceiving) strengths.

- Utilize Online Book Discovery Platforms like Goodreads or BookBub

- Write Articles or Op-eds for Online News Outlets

- Offer Personalized Book Recommendations for Readers

- Run Limited-time Promotions or Discounts

- Utilize Targeted Online Banner Advertising

- Host In-person Book Launch Events

- Develop Partnerships with Libraries for Author Talks

ESTP (Extraverted, Sensing, Thinking, Perceiving)

ESTP (Extraverted, Sensing, Thinking, Perceiving) individuals are known for their outgoing and adventurous nature, practical thinking, and adaptability. When it comes to promoting their books, they can leverage their strengths in the following ways:

Engage in personal interactions: ESTPs thrive in social settings and can make use of their extroverted nature to promote their books through personal interactions. They can attend book signings, literary festivals, and networking events to connect with readers, fellow authors, and industry professionals. By engaging in conversations and sharing their passion for their work, they can create genuine connections and generate interest in their books.

Leverage visual content: ESTPs can effectively use visual content to promote their books. They can create visually appealing book covers, promotional graphics, and engaging book trailers or videos. By capturing the attention of their audience with visually stimulating content, they can create a strong first impression and spark curiosity about their books.

Utilize social media platforms: ESTPs can maximize their presence on social media platforms that focus on visual content, such as Instagram, YouTube, and TikTok. They can showcase behind-the-scenes glimpses of their writing process, share visually captivating quotes or excerpts from their books, and engage with their audience through live videos or interactive content. By leveraging their natural charisma and ability to connect with people, they can build a strong online following and generate buzz around their books.

Seek opportunities for public speaking: ESTPs excel in public speaking engagements, and they can use this strength to promote their books. They can reach out to local libraries, book clubs, or community organizations to offer to speak about their book, share their writing journey, or provide insights into their book's themes. By delivering dynamic and engaging presentations, they can captivate their audience and generate interest in their work.

Collaborate with influencers and bloggers: ESTPs can leverage their networking skills to collaborate with influencers and popular bloggers in their book's genre or target audience. They can provide free copies of their books for reviews, interviews, or guest posts on influential blogs or podcasts. By tapping into established audiences, they can expand their reach and attract readers who trust the recommendations of their favorite influencers.

Organize contests and giveaways: ESTPs can create excitement and engagement by organizing contests and giveaways related to their books. They can offer autographed copies, merchandise, or exclusive experiences as prizes. By encouraging participation and generating buzz on social media platforms or their website, they can increase awareness of their books and create a sense of anticipation among readers.

Explore book signings at unique venues: ESTPs can think outside the traditional bookstore setting and organize book signings at unique venues that align with the themes or settings of their books. This could include hosting signings at outdoor locations, coffee shops, or themed events. By creating memorable and immersive experiences for readers, they can leave a lasting impression and generate word-of-mouth recommendations.

Engage in book-related events and conferences: ESTPs can actively participate in book-related events and conferences to network with industry professionals, attend panel discussions, and gain exposure. They can pitch their books to agents, publishers, or potential collaborators, and make connections that can further their promotional efforts. By immersing themselves in the literary community, they can expand their network and open doors to new opportunities.

Utilize storytelling and personal anecdotes: ESTPs can leverage their storytelling abilities and personal anecdotes to captivate their audience and generate interest in their books. They can share engaging stories related to their writing process, inspirations, or experiences that shaped their books. By making their personal journey relatable and intriguing, they can create a strong emotional connection with readers.

Embrace live events and book tours: ESTPs can embrace the energy of live events and embark on book tours to connect directly with their readers. They can plan engaging book launch parties, author readings, or interactive workshops. By bringing their dynamic personality and enthusiasm to these events, they can create a memorable experience for attendees and generate excitement around their books.

Share personal experiences through vlogs: ESTPs can create vlogs or video blogs to document their writing journey, book promotions, and personal experiences related to their books. They can share insights, challenges, and successes in a relatable and engaging manner. By offering a glimpse into their author life and showcasing their authentic personality, they can connect with readers on a deeper level.

Collaborate with local businesses and influencers: ESTPs can form partnerships with local businesses, influencers, or organizations that align with their book's themes or target audience. They can organize joint promotional events, create product bundles or exclusive offers, or cross-promote each other's content. By leveraging existing networks and tapping into the local community, they can expand their reach and attract new readers.

Engage in cross-promotion with other authors: ESTPs can collaborate with other authors in their genre or writing community for cross-promotion. They can participate in joint author interviews, blog tours, or book recommendation lists. By leveraging the collective fan bases and networks of fellow authors, they can increase their visibility and reach a wider audience.

Leverage your adventurous side: ESTPs can leverage their adventurous nature to create unique promotional experiences. For example, they can organize book-themed outdoor activities, scavenger hunts, or travel adventures related to their book's settings or themes. By offering readers an opportunity to engage with their books in a fun and memorable way, they can generate excitement and build a dedicated fan base.

Offer interactive content and challenges: ESTPs can create interactive content and challenges to engage their readers. This could include online quizzes, puzzles, or contests that relate to their book's characters, plot, or themes. By encouraging reader participation and providing incentives for completion, they can foster a sense of community and generate buzz around their books.

Emphasize the practical benefits of your books: ESTPs can highlight the practical benefits or actionable takeaways that readers can gain from their books. They can show-case how their books provide practical solutions, life hacks, or valuable insights that can be applied to real-life situations. By positioning their books as practical resources, they can attract readers who are looking for actionable knowledge and immediate results.

Utilize email marketing and newsletters: ESTPs can build an email list and regularly communicate with their readers through newsletters. They can share updates about their writing, exclusive content, behind-the-scenes insights, and upcoming events. By nurturing their email subscribers and providing valuable content, they can cultivate a loyal fan base and generate ongoing support for their books.

Leverage your network of friends and acquaintances: ESTPs can tap into their extensive network of friends, acquaintances, and social connections to promote their books. They can reach out to their contacts, share information about their books, and request support in spreading the word. By leveraging their social circle, they can gain initial traction and create a ripple effect in generating buzz for their books.

Stay adaptable and open to new opportunities: ESTPs thrive in dynamic environments, and it's important for them to stay adaptable and open to new promotional opportunities. They should be willing to explore emerging platforms, experiment with innovative marketing techniques, and embrace unexpected opportunities that align with their book's promotion. By staying flexible and receptive to change, they can uncover innovative ways to reach their target audience.

The following promotional activities tend to ESTP (Extraverted, Sensing, Thinking, Perceiving) strengths.

- Collaborate with Influencers or Bookstagrammers

- Run Social Media Contests or Giveaways

- Attend Local Book Signings or Author Events

- Utilize Targeted Facebook Ads Campaigns

- Host In-person Book Launch Events

- Participate in Genre-specific Conventions or Trade Shows

- Collaborate with Local Bookstores for Promotional Opportunities

ESFP (Extraverted, Sensing, Feeling, Perceiving)

ESFP (Extraverted, Sensing, Feeling, Perceiving) individuals are known for their outgoing and expressive nature, their appreciation for sensory experiences, their empathetic and compassionate approach, and their adaptability. When it comes to promoting their books, they can leverage their strengths in the following ways:

Engage in personal interactions: ESFPs thrive in social settings and can excel at promoting their books through personal interactions. They can attend book fairs, literary events, and community gatherings to connect with readers, fellow authors, and potential fans. By sharing their passion for their book and engaging in genuine conversations, they can build personal connections that foster interest and enthusiasm for their work.

Utilize social media platforms: ESFPs can make use of their natural affinity for social interaction and visual storytelling by leveraging social media platforms such as Instagram, Facebook, and Twitter. They can share engaging posts that highlight the aesthetic aspects of their book, share their writing process, or provide glimpses into the inspirations behind their work. By utilizing visually appealing content, live videos, and interactive features, they can connect with readers and create a sense of community around their book.

Create visually appealing promotional materials: ESFPs can use their eye for aesthetics to create visually appealing promotional materials such as book covers, graphics, and posters. By focusing on creating visually captivating designs that evoke emotions and intrigue, they can attract attention and generate interest in their books.

Collaborate with influencers and book reviewers: ESFPs can collaborate with influencers, book reviewers, and bloggers in their book's genre or target audience. They can provide free copies of their book for reviews, participate in interviews, or guest post on influential blogs. By leveraging the reach and credibility of these individuals, they can expand their book's visibility and tap into established communities of readers.

Organize or participate in book clubs and reading groups: ESFPs can actively engage with book clubs and reading groups that align with their book's themes or target audience. They can offer to facilitate discussions, provide insights into their writing process, or share personal anecdotes related to their book. By fostering a sense of community and actively participating in these groups, they can build a dedicated fan base and generate word-of-mouth recommendations.

Host or participate in book-related events: ESFPs can host or participate in book-related events, such as author readings, book signings, or panel discussions. They can infuse their natural charisma and enthusiasm into these events, captivating the audience and creating a memorable experience. By leaving a lasting impression, they can generate buzz and interest in their book.

Emphasize the emotional and relatable aspects of their book: ESFPs can highlight the emotional and relatable aspects of their book in their promotional efforts. They can share personal stories, discuss the book's themes and characters, and connect with readers on an emotional level. By showcasing the human experiences and feelings portrayed in their work, they can resonate with readers who value empathy and emotional connection.

Create book trailers or video content: ESFPs can leverage their expressive nature and storytelling skills by creating book trailers or video content. They can bring their book to life through visual narratives, dramatic readings, or video interviews. By engaging the senses and evoking emotions, they can capture the interest of potential readers and ignite curiosity about their book.

Utilize experiential marketing: ESFPs can create immersive and experiential marketing campaigns to promote their books. They can organize book launch parties, themed events, or interactive experiences that allow readers to engage with the world of their book. By offering memorable experiences and sensory delights, they can generate buzz and excitement among their target audience.

Share testimonials and personal endorsements: ESFPs can leverage their ESFPs can gather testimonials and personal endorsements from readers, influencers, or fellow authors who resonate with their book. They can share these endorsements on their website, social media platforms, or promotional materials. By highlighting the positive experiences and emotional impact their book has had on others, they can build credibility and attract new readers.

Create book-related visual content: ESFPs can create visually appealing content that relates to their book's themes or characters. This can include mood boards, character illustrations, or scenes inspired by their book. By sharing these visual representations, they can pique the curiosity of potential readers and create a visual connection to their story.

Leverage local communities and events: ESFPs can tap into their local communities and participate in events, festivals, or markets to promote their books. They can set up booths, engage with attendees, and create a personal connection with readers in their community. By supporting local initiatives and showcasing their work, they can generate local support and build a strong fan base.

Engage with book bloggers and online book communities: ESFPs can actively engage with book bloggers and participate in online book communities that align with their book's genre or target audience. They can offer guest posts, author interviews, or participate in book discussions. By being present in these communities and providing valuable content, they can gain visibility and attract readers who are enthusiastic about their genre.

Create an author brand that reflects their personality: ESFPs can infuse their personal brand with their vibrant personality, creating an authentic and relatable image. They can share aspects of their personal life, hobbies, or interests that align with their book's themes. By being genuine and showing readers who they are beyond their writing, they can foster a sense of connection and loyalty among their audience.

Offer exclusive behind-the-scenes content: ESFPs can provide exclusive behind-the-scenes content to their readers, offering glimpses into their writing process, inspirations, or unpublished materials. This can be shared through newsletters, social media posts, or blog updates. By providing unique insights and creating a sense of exclusivity, they can engage their readers and build anticipation for their work.

Collaborate with local businesses and venues: ESFPs can collaborate with local businesses, cafes, or venues to create mutually beneficial partnerships. They can host book-related events or readings in unique locations, collaborate on merchandise or promotional offers, or feature their books in local establishments. By leveraging the support of local businesses and venues, they can expand their reach within their community.

Foster reader engagement and interaction: ESFPs can actively engage with their readers by responding to comments, messages, and emails promptly. They can encourage readers to share their thoughts, participate in discussions, or provide feedback. By creating a welcoming and interactive environment, they can foster reader loyalty and strengthen their connection with their audience.

Share personal stories and inspirations: ESFPs can share personal stories and inspirations behind their book through blog posts, social media updates, or interviews. They can discuss the events, experiences, or emotions that led to the creation of their story. By sharing their journey and connecting on a personal level, they can intrigue readers and create a deeper connection with their work.

Stay adaptable and open to creative opportunities: ESFPs thrive in dynamic environments and should stay open to creative opportunities that may arise during their book promotion journey. They can experiment with new marketing techniques, explore collaborations with artists or musicians, or embrace unconventional approaches that align with their unique style. By staying adaptable and open-minded, they can uncover innovative ways to promote their book and captivate their audience.

Remember, these suggestions are meant to serve as a starting point, and it's important for ESFP authors to personalize their promotional strategies based on their unique strengths, target audience, and book genre. By leveraging their extraverted nature, sensory appreciation, empathy, and adaptability, ESFPs can create engaging and impactful promotional campaigns that resonate with readers and generate excitement for their books.

The following promotional activities tend to ESFP (Extraverted, Sensing, Feeling, Perceiving) strengths.

- Create a Book-themed Merchandise Line

- Run Targeted Ads on Platforms like Instagram or Pinterest

- Collaborate with Local Book Clubs or Reading Groups

- Participate in Online Book Festivals or Author Showcases

- Create Shareable and Visually Appealing Quote Images

- Collaborate with Influencers or Booktubers for Video Reviews or Recommendations

- Run Social Media Contests or Giveaways

- Attend Local Book Signings or Author Events

- Utilize Targeted Facebook Ads Campaigns

- Host In-person Book Launch Events

- Participate in Genre-specific Conventions or Trade Shows

- Collaborate with Local Bookstores for Promotional Opportunities

Chapter Twelve

Your audience and genre background

I n the previous chapters, we looked at you as the author and outlined which promotional tactics align naturally with your temperament. Now it's time to take a look at
your audience and the genre within which you write and see how we might best reach
them based on the MBTI.

Keep in mind that we have done no actual studies on how we are using the MBTI this
way, so the information presented is anecdotal at best. Use those methods that best work
for you and your writing journey. My hope is that this will at least provide you with a
launchpad to begin the process of developing a coherent marketing strategy as you review
the intersections of your audience and your own style.

It's important to remember that everyone, regardless of their MBTI type, has varied
reading preferences, making it subjective to classify books into certain MBTI kinds.
However, based on the general characteristics associated with each MBTI type, the
following hypothetical breakdown shows which MBTI types would be more drawn to
specific book categories:

ISTJ (Introverted Sensing Thinking Judging): Historical Fiction, Mystery/Thriller,
Classic Fiction

ISFJ (Introverted Sensing Feeling Judging): Romance, Literary Fiction, Biogra-
phy/Autobiography

INFJ (Introverted Intuitive Feeling Judging): Literary Fiction, Self-Help/Personal Development, Biography/Autobiography

INTJ (Introverted Intuitive Thinking Judging): Science Fiction, Fantasy, Mystery/Thriller

ISTP (Introverted Sensing Thinking Perceiving): Mystery/Thriller, Biography/Autobiography, Science Fiction

ISFP (Introverted Sensing Feeling Perceiving): Romance, Contemporary Fiction, Young Adult Fiction

INFP (Introverted Intuitive Feeling Perceiving): Literary Fiction, Fantasy, Self-Help/Personal Development

INTP (Introverted Intuitive Thinking Perceiving): Science Fiction, Fantasy, Classic Fiction

ESTP (Extraverted Sensing Thinking Perceiving): Mystery/Thriller, Biography/Autobiography, Action/Adventure

ESFP (Extraverted Sensing Feeling Perceiving): Romance, Contemporary Fiction, Cookbooks/Food and Drink

ENFP (Extraverted Intuitive Feeling Perceiving): Literary Fiction, Self-Help/Personal Development, Biography/Autobiography

ENTP (Extraverted Intuitive Thinking Perceiving): Science Fiction, Fantasy, Mystery/Thriller

ESTJ (Extraverted Sensing Thinking Judging): Mystery/Thriller, Historical Fiction, Business/Finance

ESFJ (Extraverted Sensing Feeling Judging): Romance, Contemporary Fiction, Cookbooks/Food and Drink

ENFJ (Extraverted Intuitive Feeling Judging): Literary Fiction, Self-Help/Personal Development, Biography/Autobiography

ENTJ (Extraverted Intuitive Thinking Judging): Science Fiction, Fantasy, Business/Finance

Why is this information of importance? Well, if you overlay the possible MBTI audience of the genre you are writing to, you will understand how to best promote to them based on their temperament type.

Second, you can look at your own temperament type and determine if any adjustments need to be made in your approach. For example, if you are an INTJ like me and the genre you're writing to is ESFJ. You would have to look at how you might naturally think to approach this group and make sure you incorporate in your promotion strategy more methods that appeal to the temperament of that group. Where possible, find if there are any sweet spots where both temperaments align in how they care to be approached. In this example, they both have judging in their temperament mix. So, starting with those tactics listed earlier about judging types would be a good place to begin your promotional endeavors.

This knowledge is where the approach offered in this book shines and gives you a primer to launch your marketing campaign. Because even though you might not have demographics on your specific audience you can begin knowing that your genre actually appeals to one temperament type over others and can start there as a basis to begin your marketing research, and this is a much better start than beginning at zero.

Chapter Thirteen

---

94 promotional tactics

1. Create an author website or blog to establish your online presence.

2. Build an email list of interested readers and send regular newsletters.

3. Leverage social media platforms to engage with your audience.

4. Seek endorsements from well-known authors or industry experts.

5. Use online book discovery platforms like Goodreads or BookBub.

6. Offer advanced reader copies (ARCs) for early reviews.

7. Run a pre-launch campaign to generate buzz and anticipation.

8. Participate in book fairs, conferences, and literary events.

9. Network with fellow authors, publishers, and industry professionals.

10. Create a book trailer or promotional video to showcase your book.

11. Host a virtual or in-person book launch event.

12. Submit your book for literary awards or contests.

13. Collaborate with book clubs for reading and discussion sessions.

14. Organize blog tours or virtual author interviews.

15. Seek guest posting opportunities on relevant blogs or websites.

16. Create a captivating author bio and book description.

17. Optimize your book's metadata for better discoverability on online platforms.

18. Engage with book review bloggers and offer review copies.

19. Attend local book signings or author meet-and-greets.

20. Utilize search engine optimization (SEO) techniques for your book's website.

21. Participate in podcast interviews related to your book's genre.

22. Offer exclusive bonus content or additional resources to readers.

23. Run limited-time promotions or discounts on your book.

24. Advertise your book through paid social media campaigns.

25. Guest lecture at universities or writing workshops.

26. Write articles or guest posts for relevant publications.

27. Create a book series trailer or teaser campaign.

28. Offer signed copies or personalized bookplates for readers.

29. Reach out to local bookstores for potential book signings or shelf placement.

30. Establish partnerships with non-profit organizations or charities for book donations or fundraising.

31. Utilize targeted online advertising platforms like Google Ads or Amazon Ads.

32. Write guest articles for newspapers or magazines.

33. Create a podcast related to your book's subject.

34. Run a social media contest or giveaway to engage your audience.

35. Collaborate with influencers or bookstagrammers for shoutouts or reviews.

36. Utilize online book forums and discussion platforms.

37. Create visually appealing book quote graphics for social media sharing.

38. Write articles or op-eds for online news outlets.

39. Offer discounts or incentives for readers who leave reviews.

40. Create a book series box set for increased sales potential.

41. Seek speaking engagements at conferences or industry events.

42. Create an author newsletter to keep readers updated on your writing journey.

43. Offer book signings or readings at local libraries.

44. Create a book club guide or discussion questions for readers.

45. Develop a street team or brand ambassadors to help spread the word.

46. Collaborate with book influencers on YouTube or other video platforms.

47. Write guest articles for online magazines or literary websites.

48. Create partnerships with independent bookstores or book subscription boxes.

49. Participate in online book communities or forums.

50. Host a virtual book club discussion or author Q&A session.

51. Utilize targeted online banner advertising on relevant websites.

52. Offer personalized book recommendations for readers.

53. Create a book-themed merchandise line for additional revenue streams.

54. Run targeted Facebook Ads campaigns to reach specific audience segments.

55. Leverage the power of book trailers on YouTube and other video platforms.

56. Participate in genre-specific conventions or trade shows.

57. Develop partnerships with book bloggers for promotional opportunities.

58. Utilize book review platforms like NetGalley or Edelweiss for early reviews.

59. Offer signed bookplates or bookmarks as freebies with book purchases.

60. Create a book soundtrack or playlist to enhance the reading experience.

61. Collaborate with booktubers for video reviews or recommendations.

62. Host a virtual book tour with multiple stops and author interviews.

63. Create visually appealing infographics related to your book's topic.

64. Develop an author podcast or YouTube channel to share insights and interviews.

65. Leverage the power of book subscription services for increased exposure.

66. Offer a limited edition or collector's edition of your book.

67. Create a book-themed online course or workshop for interested readers.

68. Run targeted ads on platforms like Instagram or Pinterest to reach visually oriented-readers.

69. Utilize book-themed hashtags on social media platforms for increased visibility.

70. Collaborate with local book clubs or reading groups for joint events or discussions.

71. Offer exclusive signed copies or limited-edition merchandise for loyal readers.

72. Create a book launch street team to spread the word in your local community.

73. Partner with libraries for author talks, book signings, or workshops.

74. Develop a book podcast tour, appearing as a guest on various literary podcasts.

75. Seek opportunities for cross-promotion with other authors in your genre.

76. Create shareable and visually appealing quote images for social media platforms.

77. Run targeted email marketing campaigns to reach your book's target audience.

78. Offer a special edition with bonus content or additional chapters for dedicated fans.

79. Collaborate with book reviewers or booktubers to create video review series.

80. Participate in online book festivals or virtual author showcases.

81. Create a book-specific landing page to capture reader interest and email sign-ups.

82. Develop partnerships with book-related influencers on Instagram or TikTok.

83. Offer sneak peeks or exclusive previews of upcoming books or projects.

84. Host a virtual writing workshop or webinar to share your expertise with aspiring authors.

85. Create visually stunning book trailers or animated book teasers.

86. Run targeted ads on podcast platforms to reach avid listeners.

87. Collaborate with illustrators or graphic designers for visually appealing book artwork.

88. Offer behind-the-scenes content or author vlogs on YouTube.

89. Participate in book-related hashtag challenges or trends on social media.

90. Develop partnerships with online book clubs or reading subscription services.

91. Utilize book-themed memes or humor to engage with your audience.

92. Offer bulk discounts or special packages for book clubs or bookstores.

93. Collaborate with book bloggers or influencers to host virtual book tours.

94. Stay up to date with emerging book marketing trends and adapt your strategies accordingly.

Conclusion

Keep in mind that each temperament type naturally gravitates towards those promotional tactics that align with their own temperament. However, in today's market, one must always be ready to pivot toward those promotional strategies that generate results. Be open to adopting tactics that may not be in line with your natural inclinations. Doing so might just be the one that is needed to push your book to be discovered by your best audience.

T hank you for allowing me to share my writing with you. If you enjoyed this resource and have a moment to spare, I would really appreciate a brief review on the page where you purchased the book. If you could spare a moment to leave a short review on the page where you purchased the book, I would really appreciate your help in spreading the word and making it easier for new readers to find.

Also, feel free to check out my other books on Amazon!

If you have the e-version of this book, press on the picture below to be taken to my Amazon web page!

And feel free to keep in touch with me on the following sites.

Email: tornveil@donovanmneal.com

Facebook Donovan Martin Neal

Twitter.com https://twitter.com/Donovanmneal

Instagram https://www.instagram.com/donovanmneal/

Tik Tokhttps://www.tiktok.com/@authordonovanmneal

About the Author

Donovan M. Neal is the Amazon best-selling independently published author of the Third Heaven Series: a speculative Christian fantasy four-book series that explores the captivating story of the fall of Lucifer. The book takes readers on an epic journey through the celestial realms, offering a unique perspective on the events surrounding Lucifer's rebellion and his descent into darkness.

In this imaginative tale, Donovan weaves together elements of Christian theology, angelic mythology, and fantastical world-building. The story delves into the cosmic conflict between good and evil, painting a vivid picture of the spiritual warfare that unfolded in the heavens.

Donovan has published eleven books and is currently working on publishing five more in the year 2023 alone. His books have reached thirteen countries including India, Japan, the Philippines, Mexico, Brazil, and across Europe, Canada, and the US. He has sold over thirty thousand units of his books without an agent. Donovan has produced fiction; non-fiction and most recently published a graphic novel. His genre of preference is fantasy and he has been named among notable authors such as Brian Godawa, Frank Perretti, and the late Dr. Michael S. Heiser.

When he is not imagining comic conflicts between good and evil, he serves in the prayer and discipleship ministry of his local church. You can learn more about him at **donovanmneal.com**